PROPHETIC
PASTORAL
PRACTICE

PROPHETIC PASTORAL PRACTICE

A Christian Vision of Life Together

CHARLES V. GERKIN

Abingdon Press
NASHVILLE

PROPHETIC PASTORAL PRACTICE:

A Christian Vision of Life Together

Copyright © 1991 by Abingdon Press

This book is printed on recycled, acid-free paper.

Library of Congress Cataloging-in-Publication Data

Gerkin, Charles V., 1922–
    Prophetic pastoral practice: a Christian vision ·of life together/Charles V. Gerkin.
    p.   cm.
    Includes bibliographical references and index.
    ISBN 0-687-34373-9 (pbk. : alk. paper)
    1. Pastoral theology.   2. Values.   3. Christian ethics.
I. Title.
BV4011.G4585   1991
253—dc20   90-21916
                                                         CIP

MANUFACTURED IN THE UNITED STATES OF AMERICA

FOR MY CHILDREN
Charles, Julia, Peter, Kristin, Rebecca, Rachael

CONTENTS

ACKNOWLEDGMENTS 9

INTRODUCTION: Responding Pastorally to the Signs of the
Times... 11

PART I

CHAPTER 1   Pastoral Care and the New Search for Norms........ 25

CHAPTER 2   By Reason or by the Imagination? Common Sense
and the Normative in Everyday Life.................... 48

CHAPTER 3   From Imagination to Metaphor: Pastoral Care and
the Transformation of Common Sense................ 67

PART II

CHAPTER 4   Normative Metaphors for Pastoral Work:
Presence... 91

CHAPTER 5   Normative Metaphors for Pastoral Work:
Community..116

CHAPTER 6   Normative Metaphors for Pastoral Work:
Vocation... 143

NOTES... 165

BIBLIOGRAPHY... 170

INDEX...173

ACKNOWLEDGMENTS

I t has been my good fortune for some years to have been surrounded by a community of colleagues and an institution that have been most supportive of my efforts to share my thoughts about pastoral theological concerns in writing. Emory University, particularly Candler School of Theology and its Dean, Jim L. Waits, has been most generous in providing me with the institutional support needed to do the work in the form of a modest, but significant, reduction in teaching responsibilities. Close colleagues in my own and other theological disciplines have made numerous helpful suggestions and critical comments. Most particularly, I need to express appreciation to Rodney J. Hunter, Rebecca S. Chopp, David S. Pacini, and Gary E. Myers for their reading of all or parts of the manuscript in the process of its preparation.

I have dedicated this book to my six children and thereby wish to acknowledge the quiet but constant encouragement I have received from them over the years of my professional career. Even though the things about which I write have often not been central to their own concerns, their affection and interest, which now and again bordered on admiration far beyond my deserving, have done much to keep me at the hard task of putting my thoughts into readable prose.

INTRODUCTION

RESPONDING PASTORALLY TO THE SIGNS OF THE TIMES

This book is intended for practitioners of Christian ministry in whatever context they may be serving—ministry practitioners who are puzzled and concerned about some unmistakable signals they are receiving from the people they serve in their ministerial work. Those signals indicate a climate of confusion and uncertainty. Many Christians are asking some hard questions of themselves, and of their pastors. The questions are not all alike, but they do seem to have at least one common ingredient: uncertainty about where the normative boundaries for living are now located. Or people may claim to have some pretty clear ideas about norms for living, yet be puzzled and dismayed that all around them society does not seem to conform to those norms as it once did.

Sometimes the questions they bring have to do with what is happening to their children and young people: How do I get my children to say no to drugs and alcohol? What do I say to my son or daughter when he or she reveals, with defiance or perhaps with shame and concern for his or her own welfare, that like most of his or her friends, he or she has become "sexually active"? Or, even more unsettling, how are we supposed to respond when our son or daughter reveals that he or she is homosexual? Or, in a different, but somehow related circumstance, a parishioner may request a conversation with her pastor and ask, "What am I to do? I am pregnant and I must decide if I should have an abortion. Can you help me?"

Not all of the "What should I do?" or "Is this or that right?" questions people are asking one another or their pastors, with greater urgency, are about sexuality or the boundaries to be set for young people. Those questions certainly are getting widespread attention in the media and in

11

the talk that goes on among parents. But if one listens closely to a wider range of the signs of the times, the mood of questioning and uncertainty takes on a broader dimension. If I am hearing accurately the ordinary conversations in my day-to-day contact with shopkeepers and neighbors, colleagues in church and seminary, with old and young alike, the questions about norms for ordinary life are much more general and pervasive. These questions seem to be pressing upon us wherever we look at American life. They are present in the surge of concern about violence in American family life, and on the streets of our cities.

There are echoes of these concerns on the larger scene of national and international affairs. On that larger scene, the questions about boundaries and limits are called to our attention every day by headlines disclosing the deceptive and dishonest behavior of government officials, concern over the destruction of the environment, and the danger of nuclear holocaust. For many ordinary people, however, these problems—while troubling—seem too remote and too enormous to be subject to their decision and action; except perhaps at election time, when they may have a chance to vote against a corrupt officeholder, or for a candidate who shares their concerns. Ordinarily, most people's preoccupations have more to do with everyday life and its dilemmas. Their concerns about boundaries are closer to home as they arise in relation to everything from the ethics of business life to relationships between neighbors and family members. But the fact is that, no matter where one looks in North America, the signs of the times seem unmistakable. Our culture is in flux and great controversy, while apparently in process of relocating many of the norms and boundaries that govern our common life. It is as if the common vision of the good and desirable life that was once shared by most Americans has broken into fragments so that visions of life as it "should be" have become more uncertain, frayed around the edges, and even conflicted.

REFRAMING THE CHURCH'S MINISTRY WITH REGARD TO NORMS AND BOUNDARIES

The conviction that guides the opening of this book is that the reframing of the church's efforts to address this wide-ranging set of dilemmas demands high priority for all who call themselves Christian. That reframing therefore demands high priority among those called to the church's work of ministry with, among, and by God's people in our time. The ways in which ordinary Christian people have made their decisions about norms for living—decisions often predetermined for

12

them by the generally accepted standards of popular culture—seem not to be working as well as they once did. There seem to be more questions than answers. More often than not, confusion and fragmentation of norms and boundaries for living seem to describe the situation in which Christian people find themselves.

To say that the church's efforts to address the increasingly fluid norms and boundaries need reframing is to acknowledge the church's failure to adequately and appropriately address this situation in the recent past. It is to acknowledge that the church's role in establishing and inculcating norms for living among our citizenry has been replaced in significant ways by other forms of mass communication of values and norms. In short, it is to acknowledge that the church's authority, as definer of a normative vision of human life and boundary setter for human behavior, has been badly eroded—along with the erosion of norms and boundaries in the pluralistic context of contemporary life. Much more will need to be said about that as the inquiry of this book proceeds.

GIVING PRIORITY TO PRACTICAL THEOLOGICAL INQUIRY

The inquiry to be undertaken here is best designated as a practical theological inquiry, which means that its purpose is governed by theological concerns on the one hand and by practical considerations on the other. By designating it a practical theological inquiry, I want to indicate something of the disciplinary perspective from which I approach the conversation of our mutual inquiry, and to set some parameters around the conversation. At the center of my focus is concern for the practical work of ministry to persons as individuals and as members of church communities. So at one level this book is intended as an inquiry into practical theology for ministry practice. At a second level, however, the discussion will inquire into the day-to-day normative, visionary, and boundary-setting practices of the people of the church who find their Christian presence and vocation in the larger society increasingly influenced by a pluralism of values, norms, and visions of the good life, not all of which are compatible with a Christian perspective. At yet a third level, therefore, the ordinary practices of that larger human cultural community in which the church is set, and within which it must carry out its ministry to the world, must be taken into consideration. At each of those levels there are questions of norms and visional boundaries that have become increasingly urgent and difficult.

Readers familiar with my earlier book, *Widening the Horizons: Pastoral*

13

Responses to a Fragmented Society, will remember that I argued there that the radically pluralistic situation in American culture in our time presents the Christian community with both a problem and an opportunity.[1] The risk and danger of radical pluralism is of fragmentation: the creation of a society that has lost its sense of direction and unity concerning values and normative practices. The opportunity is that, in a situation of norms and values flux, some of the reified values and oppressively constricting boundaries that have brought harm to some members of the society may be broken open and become subject to creative transformation.

A more unified society than ours is tends to instill in its young a set of normative values that, once learned through socialization, is thereafter taken for granted. To be sure, some of those values and norms may be faulty or skewed to the advantage of some, and the oppressive disadvantage of others. But a degree of consensus about those values does maintain a certain unity in the society. The society that is rife with pluralism is in a very different situation. Socialization processes begin to break down or take a very different form. Individualism, sub-grouping, and competition of values begin to break up the normative control of consensual values.

As Robert Bellah and his associates have carefully documented in their widely read book *Habits of the Heart*, North American society has, from its beginning, been heavily influenced by the tradition of individualism. This highly valued tradition of individual freedom has, in the American experience, been historically counterbalanced by deep loyalties to a more communal, covenantal tradition that for most Americans can be traced back to its biblical sources.[2] With the rapid increase of pluralism in current American society, however, an increasingly heavy emphasis on individualism and choice of what has come to be called "life-style" has developed. Coupled with our society's increasing dependence on the mass media and the breakdown of community life in our cities, that emphasis has caused the balance between consensus and individualism to become more and more tenuous. The result is that our society has become a virtual marketplace of values and norms that often conflict, and is composed of a multiplicity of identity-shaping clusters of human activity that compete for individual investment of energy and loyalty. Meanwhile, there are a growing number of indications that many in the society of pluralism and individualism are searching, sometimes in odd ways, to rediscover a sense of community and consensus.

In a situation of cultural fragmentation, normative questions—both individual and corporate—are often resolved by default. Normative questions remain unexamined, while decisions are made on pragmatic grounds of expediency and/or under the duress of economic or social survival considerations. Individuals caught in such a socio-cultural morass of unacknowledged value contradictions and pressures may get swept along with the fluctuating currents of popular value faddism and/or felt demands from the authorities of the working world. Under duress from conflicting expectations of differing reference groups, many simply fall into living by a survival psychology in the outside, communal world while trying to retain whatever integrity they can in their private lives.

Such a situation likewise leaves many persons vulnerable to invitations from the religious right to "return to old-time values" while narrowing the scope of value issues about which to be concerned. A common result of response to those invitations is that individual and communal moral concern becomes constricted to a short list of issues such as abortion, homosexuality, and marital infidelity, while other significant normative issues—issues often more crucial to the welfare of the society—are ignored. Religion then takes a sharp turn to the right and the imagined past, while the issues of peace and justice, the ethics of business and industry, and the formation of a more human community go unaddressed.

For the pastoral care and counseling practitioner, the cultural value fragmentation I have alluded to presents the necessity of gaining clarity concerning the normative vision that is to guide the pastor's, and the religious community's, ministry to persons. Said very simply, pastors and lay persons need to gain greater clarity about just what sort of human beings we are seeking to help persons become under our care. It is no longer enough for the pastoral care practitioner simply to appropriate the various techniques of the secular helping professions that have sprung up during the twentieth century as models for pastoral work with persons having difficulty with the stresses and strains of living in the present society. Though these techniques are at times quite useful, they are incapable of undergirding the central purposes of a ministry that seeks to embody the meanings and values that have shaped the Christian tradition over time. These techniques also are incapable of supporting a ministry to persons caught up in a culture that is suffering from the malaise of norms and boundaries fragmentation. That undergirding must be derived from the core values and meanings rooted in the primary texts of the Christian narrative tradition.

UNDERGIRDING PREMISES

The work of this book will involve both inquiry and argument. As inquiry, our work will be to see if the manifest problems of norms and

15

boundaries fragmentation can be broken open to see what underlies and shapes those problems. As argument, the book will seek to carry out the inquiry and make pastoral response proposals that grow out of a certain model: the model of narrative hermeneutical practical theology. As the reader will see, that model shapes the inquiry and the argument in certain ways, and resists shaping it in other ways that may have value. A model always tends to cause the user of the model to see things in a certain way and to project a certain trajectory to the inquiry it structures. The model here presented is a particularly appropriate one for Christian pastoral work in that it takes very seriously the normative grounding of the Christian community in the biblical and Christian theological tradition. But it takes equally seriously the contemporary situation in American society. It is, therefore, presented as a model that is both true to the Christian faith, and practical in the work of ministry as pastors seek to be agents of transformation in the contemporary church and world.

Although disclosure of the model and its ramifications will need to await the unfolding of the inquiry it shapes on the ensuing pages, it may be useful to the reader to glimpse some of the undergirding premises on which the book is based. Consider what follows, then, as a general and informal skeletal framework of theses or preunderstandings that will guide the inquiry.

1. Metaphorical and imagistic values and meanings.

The central values and meanings that have shaped the normative understanding of the Christian life, and therefore the goals of pastoral ministry, have historically been fundamentally metaphorical and imagistic. The Christian community has sustained itself over centuries of time by maintaining its loyalty to the biblical collection of stories and other writings that tell of the coming into being of a people who saw themselves as the people of God whose primary relationship was to that God, who brought them into being and sustained their life. By the use of analogy, metaphor, and symbol, the people called Christian have attempted over the centuries to live their lives according to that primal narrative. In doing so, they often have been stubbornly wrongheaded and fallen short of the vision of "life under God" or "life in Christ" that the narrative sought to convey. Often, they have acted only on fragmentary and even distorted perceptions of what the story contains. Yet, the Christian community, through the centuries, has sustained its identity through the appropriation and reappropriation of the images, themes, and metaphors of that biblical narrative. For Christians it contains a normative vision of what life is and should be.

16

To say that the biblical and Christian narrative contains a normative vision of what life is and should be is to suggest that there is a certain aesthetic ethic—an aesthetic vision of the good, the true, and the beautiful—that has been powerfully operative in the Christian community's self understanding. In certain important ways, the life of Christians together—and the life of Christians in relation to the larger world of human affairs—was to be modeled after that vision. Wisdom about human affairs was to be guided by the wisdom found in the biblical narratives and teachings.

2. Biblical values are appropriated by living life according to the image of the good life presented by the biblical story.

Although the normative values and meanings that took form in the biblical, and later Christian, narratives may be objectified and argued philosophically and theologically in the language of logic and reason, they are more often appropriated by ordinary persons not by logical argument or by the rule of reason, but metaphorically and in the manner of living life according to the governance of a story that portrays certain images of the good life. Ordinary persons, insofar as they see themselves as Christians, thus tend to live their lives according to some vision of what the Christian life is for them. Stated again in philosophical terms, that means that ordinary people, most often quite unselfconsciously, tend to follow a fundamentally intuitive, and at times unexamined, aesthetic ethic—an aesthetic vision of the good and Christian life that they carry with them in their imagination. That aesthetic vision is greatly influenced by the commonly held aesthetics of the good life of the broader culture in which these individuals live. The vision of the good life disclosed in the biblical and Christian narratives, and the vision operative in, for example, middle-class North American culture, are often so fused in the imaginations of many Americans that they are almost indistinguishable. In short, they also are rooted in an aesthetic vision of the individual and communal life that the work of pastoral ministry is intended to foster and demonstrate.

3. The norms that set the direction for pastoral ministry with persons are, like the norms for living, fundamentally metaphorical and imagistic.

That means that caregivers likewise have an understanding of what it means to be a person living a fully human life within the norms of Christian personhood and of what a fully human and Christian community should be. While that vision may have been modified by more or less careful academic study of fields such as theological ethics and developmental and social psychology, nevertheless the core vision of the good individual and corporate life of the pastoral practitioner remains, in fundamental ways, imagistic and metaphorical. Furthermore, the vision of the good and Christian life is best communicated to persons by the caregiver in the language of metaphor, image, and narrative, on the one hand, and of relationship, attitude, and behavior, on the other hand. These latter behavioral manifestations of the caregiver's vision function in important ways as metaphors, that is, they either so function or fail to function to make a metaphorical connection between the situation and relationships at issue and the normative vision of the fully human and Christian life.

This way of speaking of the pastoral relationship with persons and communities does not, of course, rule out the use of a language of moral or ethical reasoning on the part of pastors as they go about their work. There are often occasions when the use of such language will no doubt be helpful to the persons with whom the pastor is working. Likewise, it does not rule out the use of the language of therapeutics and psychological intervention on occasion. That language can also, at times, be both pragmatically useful and disclosive of aspects of the primary aesthetic vision that governs pastoral work. But, in the model for pastoral work being developed here, these languages are always in some sense secondary to the primary work of ministry with persons and communities that makes use of metaphor, image, symbol, and narrative theme to assist persons in making the metaphorical connection between the situations of their lives and the grounding narratives of the tradition by which they are named as Christians.

4. Retrieving and reinterpreting biblical metaphors and images.

As has already been suggested, the core metaphors and images that set the direction for pastoral ministry and govern its intended outcomes are to be found in the core, or root, metaphors found in the biblical narrative and further developed in Christian theological tradition. Retrieval of those meanings, however, inevitably involves reinterpretation in order to relate those meanings to the specifics of the contemporary situation in which the pastor is working. In doing the work of retrieval, the contemporary pastor or care giver must give appropriate attention to the problems of interpretation resulting from the manner in which the cultural appropriation of those meanings in the remote or more recent past has inevitably involved varying degrees of distortion, error, and misappropriation. As Paul Ricoeur suggests, therefore, the retrieval of core metaphorical meanings, and of meanings found in contemporary situations as well, needs to be done with an appropriate degree of suspicion.[3]

It should be kept in mind that, within the model being developed in this book, the interpretation and reinterpretation of a tradition such as the biblical and Christian tradition is a continuous, living, dynamic process. The goal is not to arrive at the one *exact, forever true* understanding of the core meanings of the tradition in some ahistorical sense. Rather, in this model, traditions are living, historical processes in which meanings, although rooted in primary images and symbolic metaphorical themes, continually interact with the changing situations of history to create new and highly nuanced understandings of their implications. The work of ministry in making the metaphorical connections between the core narratives and the narratives being enacted in contemporary living situations is thus a significant part of sustaining the life and vitality of the tradition to which ministry attempts to be loyal. Without such continual reinterpretation and metaphorical enactment, the Christian tradition would quickly become a dead tradition, unrelated to the problems and dilemmas of ongoing human life.

5. Tending the dialogical relationship: the "fusion of horizons."

While remaining faithful to these core normative metaphors and images in pastoral work, the ministry practitioner—as representative of the Christian story and its tradition—will likewise remain faithful in his or her respect for the particularity of the persons and human situations with which the pastor is confronted. Thus, good pastoral work always entails a dialogical relationship between the issues and problems involved in the particular human situation at hand and the core metaphorical values and meanings of the Christian story. Pastoral work virtually always involves tending this dialogical relationship in which both the particularity of the situation at hand and the horizon of meaning contained in the Christian story become open to reassessment, reevaluation, and reinterpretation. Attending to this dialogue is therefore best described as a hermeneutical (interpretive) task in the double sense of interpretation of core images and metaphors of the Christian tradition and interpretation of the particularity of contemporary situations with which the pastor is confronted. It is by means of a process that, following Gadamer, I would label as a *fusion of horizons* of those two interpretations that pastoral work can best be grounded in the core meanings of the Christian narrative of the world.

Since the adaptation of Gadamer's concept of the fusion of horizons in my earlier work is crucial to the theoretical argument undergirding this book, it will perhaps be useful to explicate that concept briefly. Gadamer first put forward the concept of the fusion of horizons as part of his proposal concerning the interpretation of written texts and other human artifacts. The term *horizon* is a metaphor drawn from physical geographic space. It points to whatever can be seen from a certain standpoint, a particular vantage. Simply stated, the concept suggests that every humanly constructed text or artifact, be that a biblical text or an art object, emerges from, and is an expression of, a horizon of understanding or meaning. Likewise, the person who seeks to understand or interpret a text or artifact lives within and is constituted by a horizon of meaning. Thus, the would-be interpreter does not come to the interpretive task empty handed or with an absolutely open mind. Rather, the interpreter comes with certain preunderstandings—*prejudices* in Gadamer's language. Yet the interpreter's desire is to allow the text or artifact to speak to the interpreter out of its own horizon.

In the act of interpretation, a dialogical relationship is initiated that involves a meaning exchange between interpreter and text. In Gadamer's view, as that dialogue proceeds, the dialogue itself takes over and a process he termed the *fusion of horizons* begins to take place. The meanings that emerge from that fusion are historical, that is, they are unique to that historical interpretive occasion. It is in the continuing process of the fusion of horizons between classic texts of a tradition and interpreters who come with differing, historically shaped horizons that a tradition remains alive and viable in differing situations over time. Without such a process of fusion of horizons, a tradition becomes fixed and deadened; its power to speak to the changing scene of historical existence is lost.[4]

The adaptations of Gadamer's concept of the fusion of horizons made in my earlier books were at several levels. First, in *The Living Human Document* I proposed that the individual self, in the course of its development, creates a narratively constructed horizon of meaning concerning itself and the world in which it finds itself. That horizon is the result of countless fusions with the familial, socio-cultural, and faith tradition horizons encountered by the individual. Furthermore, I proposed that the encounter between a person seeking help with the common problems of living and the one seeking to be helpful (within the purpose of that book, the pastoral counselor), there develops a dialogical process best understood as a fusion of horizons analogous to the process Gadamer describes. The horizon of the help-seeker and that of the helper interact and fuse in ways that may bring about alterations in the meaning horizon of both helper and help-seeker.

In *Widening the Horizons*, I further expanded the adaptation of the fusion of horizons concept to encompass the tasks of ministry within a faith community seeking to be faithful to the central meanings of the Christian tradition. The metaphor *widening the horizons* as utilized in that book refers both to the task the book undertook to broaden and deepen the scope of concern and involvement of pastors in their pastoral work, and to the role of ministry in widening the horizons of persons and congregations under the care of the pastor. In that book, the role of the pastor in pastoral work was formulated as the role of interpretive pastoral guidance.

6. The hermeneutic phenomenology of Gadamer and Ricoeur.

By placing the emphasis on interpretation of root images and metaphors, and on contemporary situations, I am locating the methodological approach to be developed in this book within a particular stream of philosophical inquiry. The model of normative reflection to be developed in this book is, methodologically speaking, rooted in philosophical hermeneutics, most particularly the hermeneutic phenomenology of Hans-Georg Gadamer and Paul Ricoeur.[5] The choice to locate the approach within this philosophical stream is a practical one. In the work of the pastor with ordinary persons, it is necessary to get beneath the level of cognitive or reasonable logic to a level of experience that encompasses the intuitive, the emotional and affective life, and the relational affinities that emerge more from individual and communal living out of a story carried in the person's imagination than they do from intellectual reasoning and/or logical disputation.

In other words, ordinary persons do not live primarily by the rule of reason narrowly conceived, nor do they make their decisions and choices or form their relationships primarily by means of a logical process that can best be described as practical moral reasoning.[6] That means that pastoral care and counseling as ministering response to persons where they live and make their decisions must be prepared to discern the presence of normative issues as they appear in ordinary human language—namely the language of relationship, image, metaphor, and story—and to reflect with persons within our care in those genres of language. There are simply levels of experience that cannot be spoken of in conversation in any other way than by the way of story, image, and metaphor.

7. Metaphorical theology.

One final introductory comment will perhaps be helpful to the reader in his or her journey through the six chapters that follow. The emphasis laid on image, metaphor, and story in the book places the pastoral theology with which I am working within the contemporary stream of theological thought that has been given the designation *metaphorical theology*.[7] That stream of contemporary theology builds on the assumption that no one metaphor (e.g., metaphors such as God as Redeemer, or humans as God's children or as co-creators with God) is adequate to convey the rich and varied meanings of Christian understanding. Rather, a rich variety of metaphors and images are both necessary and to be found within the biblical narrative. Because the book will build upon a selection of grounding metaphors—none of which alone is adequate, and all of which originate in the biblical narrative—the pastoral theology undertaken here will be developed as a metaphorical, narrative pastoral theology.

We begin our inquiry in chapter 1 with an effort to understand the recent historical and cultural process that has brought us to the time of norms and boundaries confusion and fragmentation that our society is experiencing. The remainder of part one will develop the model, the skeleton of which has been sketched out in the Introduction. Part two of the book will then delve into several of the core metaphors of the biblical narrative, the reappropriation of which seems particularly crucial in our present situation.

PART ONE

CHAPTER ONE

PASTORAL CARE AND THE NEW SEARCH FOR NORMS

T he business executive sitting across the room from me was an old friend and former counselee of mine. In his middle years, he had worked for the same company since completing a graduate professional degree. I knew him not only as an active churchman, but also as one who had on occasion expressed his agnostic thoughts about the viability of the Christian world view. I knew him also as one who, while attaining some success in the business world, had frequently harbored misgivings about whether the vocation he had chosen, somewhat by default as a young man, was really suited to his personality. But he had worked hard, achieving an affluence in his life-style that few in the business world attain.

He had come to see me to talk about a recent experience in his work that had left him with troubled thoughts. He began the story by reminding me that, as he says is the case all across the business world, the leadership of the company had in recent years passed to some of the younger members of the firm who, by their driving ambition and aggressive business tactics had moved into positions of leadership formerly attained largely by processes of accumulated seniority. The story he told me was of a high level executive committee meeting of the firm that one of his superiors who was out of town had asked him to attend. With considerable passion he spoke of a meeting where, in language filled with obscenities and the language of the street, fellow members of the company who were not present were discussed with "ruthless disregard for either truth or respect for the dignity of one's fellow workers." Not only that, but several important decisions were made concerning business matters that disregarded all considerations save the notorious bottom line of potential for profit.

25

In a tone mixed with sadness and anger, my friend reported his shock and dismay in realizing how the actuality of the way the business of the company was being carried on cut like a knife across the images in his mind of how good business transactions should be carried out. He said he had found himself recalling experiences he had had as a young boy with a gang of kids trying to act tough. "Chuck, they were like a bunch of kids playing like they were men and overacting the role! I wondered what had happened to things like respect, sincerity, gentility in human affairs. And this is the firm I work for and from which I get my paycheck!"

From our past relationship, I knew something of my old friend's hard-won integrity, the fundamental probity of his character. I was therefore not surprised by his reaction to his observation of the inner workings of the higher levels of his business community. In the conversation that followed, we considered together whether what he had seen and heard had been simply an aberration or whether he had caught a glimpse of something that was becoming pervasive in American business and political life.

What follows on these pages will argue not only that what this circumspect businessman observed with dismay was indeed a glimpse into an increasingly pervasive phenomenon of our time in Western culture, but also that the questions the experience evoked in him and in me as listener are also common among many people in American society. I will argue that we live in a time of fragmentation of commonly accepted boundaries and norms and a concomitant new search for norms, images, and visions of the good by which day-to-day human relationships are to be governed. Where are the boundaries? What are the rules and appropriate guiding visions for human business and social affairs? Are there any longer such norms and images that we and our fellow citizens can so agree on that we can take them for granted? These were my friend's questions. I found as we talked together that they were mine, as well. I believe they are questions that have profound pertinence for the work of ministry among God's people in our time.

A RANDOM SAMPLING OF SIGNS OF THE TIMES

In the course of a number of months of preparation for the writing of this book, I found myself collecting a growing list of vignettes of everyday life that clustered around the observations and concerns my businessman friend and I had discussed. I offer a few of them here as a sampling to which I would predict my readers could add innumerable experiences of their own.

1. The Iran-Contra Affair

What came to be known as the "Iran-Contra Affair" dominated the headlines of daily newspapers across America for an entire summer in 1987, and lingered in the public consciousness for many months to follow. The proceedings related to it in the nation's capital became what many commentators referred to as the great American soap opera that attracted millions of ordinary Americans to their television screens. Did or did not the principals in that bizarre episode in American foreign relations violate the laws of the land? Were their acts justifiable, even heroic, or were they instead reprehensible to the point of demanding appropriate disgrace and punishment? Where are the boundaries that govern what should and should not be done in the national interest? Debates, not only carried on by the nations' leaders, but also on the street corners and in the press, seemed erratic and fragmentary during that period. Images of a nation divided about matters of honesty and openness in government, the importance of truth as opposed to the masking of behavior by pretense and cover-up, were apparent everywhere. Where are the boundaries that ought to govern such matters? Are there norms for behavior of governments that differ from norms for individuals and private groups? On and on the questions tossed to and fro, speaking of a people no longer certain of societal rules.

2. Standards for sexuality

Another arena of vital interest and concern, yet one upon which the American public appears equally divided and preoccupied, is the social and moral crisis in relation to the apparent breakdown of traditional standards with regard to sexuality. What are the boundaries that should govern relationships between the sexes? Should those boundaries be publicly and consensually prescribed, even enforced, or are they to be set only within the structure of common consent of the participants? And how are we as a people to set standards concerning homosexuality, now that the homosexual community has emerged from the closet of secrecy into the light of public acknowledgment? What about AIDS? Does that scourge that first struck the homosexual community—only subsequently to spread to affect heterosexuals, their children, and people who were neither homosexuals nor drug abusers—alter the considerations that are to govern public and private attitudes and standards in sexual affairs? Where are the norms for sexuality in an age of blatant, open discussion

27

and erratic behavior that is so apparently governed by equally blatant disagreement concerning the rules of the human sexual game? The condoms have been moved from under the back counters of America's drug stores and the coin machines hidden in the men's rooms of filling stations along our highways. They now occupy open display cases, not only in the pharmacies of our cities, but also in grocery and discount stores. The boundaries have certainly changed with regard to such things, but where are they now located?

Reflecting on those questions brings to my remembrance another quick vignette of recent experience. I recall one day coming out of the university student center on the campus where I teach, following lunch in the faculty dining room. In my path was a table set up by what appeared to be a student advocacy group. On the table rested a hand-lettered poster sign that read: "SAFE SEX IS A FANTASY. MANDATORY TESTING, QUARANTINE, IMMUNIZATION."

I thought of the built-in implications of that sign and was confronted with the wrenching awareness that the search for boundaries among young college students had taken an odd twist. "Quarantine the AIDS victims! Immunize us all, so we can again have safe and random sex!" Where indeed are the boundaries? What are the norms that govern our expression of sexuality?

3. Whose crime? Whose punishment?

Finally, and somewhat with tongue in cheek, I would suggest that it might be worth reflecting on the cultural implications of a little vignette of Americana that appeared in the daily newspaper not long ago. The report was of a pending lawsuit in Oakland, California, brought by a convicted robber against the city and the savings and loan association that he had robbed of two million dollars. The suit brought by the robber claimed that he suffered "excruciating pain when a bundle of cash exploded in his pants." The robber was insisting that the bank should have known that the booby trap planted in the money would have devastating effects. He suffered second and third degree burns as he fled the bank and wanted to be compensated for his pain! Where, indeed, are the boundaries?

THE NORMATIVE LEADERSHIP TASK OF THE CHURCH

I offer this sampling of vignettes of contemporary life as but a few of the virtual plethora of signs of the times, large and small in their

28

individual significance, that can be observed at every level of our social life. Taken together, these events and conflicts signal the fragmentation of norms and boundaries in North American society. They indicate confusion and controversy concerning the vision that is to guide American culture's common life. To take those signs of the times seriously means to acknowledge that we live in a time of blurred boundaries, of push and pull toward one norm or another in often confusing ways.

The multifaceted question the readers of this book are asked to pursue with me can be stated in a number of ways. In such a time as this, What does it mean to give pastoral guidance to God's people? How are the firm groundings of good and evil to be reestablished in American society? Can the old boundaries ever be reestablished? Or is it possible that the norms and visions of the good that undergird human relationships and actions need to be entirely reenvisioned? Do we need a whole new set of norms that, rather than coming from the historic sources of our religious tradition, emerge from the conditions of modern (or, for some, post-modern) life? For pastoral and lay leaders of the churches alike, all these questions converge around the question as to how we who are called to be pastoral and lay ministry leaders go about the task of giving purposive guidance to the people of God.

These questions that arise from reflection on the signs of our times are not only multifaceted, they are multilayered, as well. They do not ask only the grounding question as to how normative meanings are to be adjudicated, or how and on what basis normative standards for human conduct are to be established. The root questions they contain are also, at a fundamental level, theological and anthropological. They raise the basic questions concerning the purpose of God in creation and the nature and purpose of the human as creature, subject to God's purpose in creation. At another level, they also ask how the most fundamental questions of good and evil arise in the ordinariness of everyday life. How are we to understand the way ordinary people, most often unschooled in the disciplines of rigorous theological or ethical thinking, actually appropriate norms, boundaries, and visions of the good for their behavior? And, as I have already suggested, there is yet another layer of questions at the level of ministry methodology. Once we come to some conclusion about what norms, boundaries, and visions of the good, the true, and the beautiful *ought* to govern human life in community, how are these boundaries to be established in the consensus of the people?

This latter group of questions is currently receiving renewed attention on the part of ministry theorists. Perhaps this attention is not only in response to the recognition of the fragmentation of norms that characterizes contemporary life in so-called First World societies, but also because of the surge of revolutionary and liberationist consciousness among the peoples of the Third World, and among women. There is a renewed awareness of the role of actual practices in shaping and reshaping norms and governing visions. Traditionally stated norms as they have actually been practiced have been uncovered so as to reveal that the practices emerging from them have often resulted in subtle or more blatant distortions, indeed violations, of the root meanings of those norms themselves. One result of this newfound awareness is a resurgence of interest in the problem of human practices at a number of levels. Commonly accepted ways of thinking abut the distinctive roles of theory, including theological/ethical theory, and practice are being challenged on all sides.

Although careful study of key figures in the development of the theological tradition during the nineteenth and early twentieth centuries will reveal predominant interest in the primacy of human practices for theological construction, the common way of approaching questions of theory and practice issues in theological education and the teaching of ministry practice methodology in America has, until quite recently, tended to follow the pattern of giving a certain priority to theory. First, by means of careful biblical, theological, and ethical reflection, emphasis has been placed on establishing normative principles and rules on the basis of which norms and boundaries for human practices *ought* to be established. Once that has been achieved, the questions of application in practice have tended to follow as secondary questions of applied theory.

The renewal of interest in practice and the place of practical theology in theological work has, however, brought forth the question as to whether this traditional way of mapping an approach to practical normative problems is not flawed. Is it a matter of first deciding what the norms and boundaries should be, and then asking the questions about application? Is it not more nearly the case that decisions about what norms should apply, and how those norms are to be engendered in the lives of people, must emerge from the crucible of reflective engagement of human practices, whether those be the practices of lay people in their ethical and boundary setting decision making, or the practices of concrete pastoral work?

As one who, for a lifetime, has been immersed in the practice and teaching of pastoral care and counseling, by natural bent and established habit of mind I come at these questions with primary interest in the issues of ministry practices. Accordingly, it is to the questions that in theological studies are most often placed at the end of the inquiry that my mind quite automatically turns. How do ordinary people go about making decisions concerning norms and boundaries? How do they live out their internalized visions of the good life in relation to the mundane tasks and choices of everyday life? Where do they turn when they are confronted with situations in the course of their ordinary living that contain the issues of norms and boundaries? Do they make those decisions by the logical process of careful theological/ethical reasoning, the exercise of critical thought? Do they self-consciously appropriate biblical or other traditional religious norms? Or do they, in their actual practices, engage in a process less disciplined, more informal, and unreflective than that? If that is the case, how might that process best be understood, and can our understanding of that process shed any light on the questions concerning pastoral guidance of God's ordinary people in a time of boundary fragmentation?

Such questions should be the governing questions of ministry practices, because it is the practical, down-to-earth problems of norms, boundaries, and the enacting of visions as ordinary people encounter them that provide the force behind the new search for norms and boundaries that will function in a fragmented social situation. As the Roman Catholic theologian David Tracy has said in his book, *Plurality and Ambiguity*, "A good historian, perhaps more than any other thinker or artist, can most clearly demonstrate the truth of the observation that though life is reflected upon through general ideas, it is always lived in the details."[1] Although Tracy's observation is, within the context of his book, almost made as an off-hand remark, it is an important one for the argument to be developed. Paraphrased only slightly to fit the present context, the observation about the importance of the details of life underlines the importance of a comparable observation, namely, that it is in the ordinary choices and decisions made by ordinary people—the details of daily living—that societal norms and visions of the good life will either function as governing rules and visions for living or will, in the long term, be called into question. Socio-cultural norms and cultural visions exercise their governing authority within a society only as they become predominantly consensual among the mass of ordinary people of the society. As the social historian Russell Jacoby has rightly phrased it, "The social does not 'influence' the private; it dwells within it."[2] Furthermore, it is at this level of the details of private life and decision-making that the social problems become visible to pastoral and lay church leaders in ways that can prompt fresh inquiry concerning cultural norms.

CAUSES OF BOUNDARY FRAGMENTATION

In the course of assimilating such signs of the times as my random list of vignettes of American life suggests, one cannot help asking: "Why is this

31

the case? What is the reason for the fragmentation of the taken-for-granted norms for ordinary living and the consensual visional boundaries within which the affairs of our common life are to be managed? What are the social and psychological roots of our uncertainty about norms that seems so pervasive?" Awareness of the social condition in which we find ourselves demands investigation into the archaeology that lies beneath the frenetic surface of our cultural behavior.

Although the present writing prohibits an exhaustive probing of the historical, social, and psychological antecedents of the erosion of solid consensus with regard to a vision of the good life in the American experience, it is crucial to the constructive proposals that I make in later chapters that appropriate attention be given here to several different but related factors that lie behind our present situation. Some of these factors are highly visible in public, social, and political life so that they have become matters of political controversy. Others are less visible in the give and take of public argument, but nevertheless have operated powerfully to break open long-held customary patterns of social practice and ways of envisioning the ideal life toward which the common life of the people should be directed. Taken together, these factors seem to have so torn the fabric of common consent in American popular culture as to make for a fractured normative skeletal vision that no longer supports a consensual body of opinion and lived practice in the details of our common life.

Consider, then, the following list of social processes that factor into the engendering of the present visional fragmentation:

1. The resurgence of American individualism, now largely psychologized, that has resulted in the "age of the self."

The American tradition of individualism—with its placing of premium value on the right of the individual to "life, liberty, and the pursuit of happiness"—has been one of the cornerstones of American self-understanding from colonial times. As Robert Bellah and his associates have documented, that icon of the American character has functioned from the beginning as both a legitimation of individual resistance to the setting of too tight boundaries around individual choice, and as a normative principle to be incorporated in all efforts to set boundaries for social practices.[3] Although most often held in tension with other, more communally grounded governing images of what the common life of Americans should embody, the image of individual freedom to decide and act for oneself has—from the beginning—made for a certain cultural uneasiness and pluralism concerning rules, boundaries, and enculturated visions of the good, the true, and the beautiful.[4]

American individualism in the twentieth century has undoubtedly taken a strongly psychological turn. Consensually held boundaries to govern individual and corporate behavior have been powerfully countered by equally consensually held expectations of self-actualization and self-expression. The seeds of this strong turn toward self-fulfillment were already nascently present in such phenomena as the Emmanuel Movement at the turn of the century[5] and the popular appropriation of the psychologist William James' classic study of individual religion, *The Varieties of Religious Experience.*[6] It was not, however, until the rise of the mental health movement following World War II, and the accompanying surge of interest in the promise of psychotherapeutic release of individuals from whatever inhibited them from full exercise of self-expression, that the psychological mode of resurgence of individualism became full blown on American cultural life.[7] Individuals in American society began to feel increasingly free to question the rule of conventional values and relational stereotypes. Breathing space for exercise of idiosyncratic choice that better fit the perceptions and propensities of the individual's own understanding began to be valued and claimed by more and more people who felt, as the common saying went, "freed up" to be themselves.

This freeing of American individual psychological autonomy by the psychologizing of individualism undoubtedly had important salutary effects, most particularly among middle-class Americans. Many conventionalisms and moralisms were opened up for questioning and reexamination. In that process, many of the conventionalities in American religious life likewise were opened to a process of reexamination. As the modern pastoral care and counseling movement gathered momentum in the churches through the appropriation of psychological and psychotherapeutic ways of thinking in ministry to individuals and families, many pastors and lay Christians began to break out of the constrictions of religious piety grounded in guilt and conformity. A new spirit of grace and freedom began to permeate American religious life, particularly in the mainline, liberal Protestant churches.

While the influence of the thrust of psychologized individualism on the ministry and relational ethos of the American churches had a freeing effect, it also deeply influenced both clerical and popular lay understanding of the ambiguities and deep blockages to the realization of human individual and relational desire. By appropriating psychological and psychoanalytic ways of thinking concerning the power of unconscious motivations, ambivalence, and interpersonal conflict, countless Christians were enabled to renew their understanding of the doctrinal and moral traditions of the faith concerning human fault and propensity for sin in enlivened ways. Moral concerns that had threatened to be reduced to moralisms began to be opened up to greater emphasis on the meaning and possibility of relational integrity and authenticity.

For some in the churches, however, the appropriation of psychological ways of thinking took a different and more radical turn away from human limitations and need for controls, toward preoccupation with unencumbered human possibilities. Particularly among adherents to the humanistic psychologies who joined what came to be called the human potential movement, a decidedly romantic valuing of individual choice and individual fulfillment reigned supreme.[8]

As the therapeutic culture, so critically documented by Philip Rieff in his *The Triumph of the Therapeutic* in the mid-sixties, joined in confluence with other powerful societal movements of the sixties, the cultural atmosphere of the "age of the self" became increasingly antinomian and litigious with regard to norms and boundaries in human affairs.[9] The crude, but popular slogans, "Do your own thing!" and "Sue the bastards!" signaled a society more and more bent on the assertion of individually held perceptions of value, and the use of the legal power structures of the society to contend for the right to act on one's own point of view. Like Sandberg's fog that creeps with cat feet across the land, an increasingly antinomian and *laissez faire* atmosphere—with regard to norms and visions of the good life—settled upon American culture.

2. The growing realization that began to penetrate popular culture in the mid–twentieth century concerning the oppression that had resulted from the dominant control of many traditional norms.

Tradition as a taken-for-granted way of life whose norms for living are largely unquestioned has, during the latter half of the twentieth century, been buffetted more and more strenuously by the forces of revision. Though these gathering winds of change have blown from several diverse directions, creating a virtual whirlwind of reform, a common perception provided much of the energy behind their movement. From all sides grew the clamor of dissent from traditional patterns that governed day-to-day life that were perceived as oppressive and unjust.

The spearhead of revolt against dominant societal norms that powerfully altered commonly accepted boundaries for human relationships was undoubtedly the black civil rights movement of the 1950s and 1960s. White domination of the black minority by both law and custom was unmasked as white injustice and cruel white prejudice. The boundaries that separated the races from one another began to crumble one by one. As the civil rights movement, led largely by black church leaders such as Martin Luther King, Jr., gathered momentum, the hypocrisy beneath much of popular Christian setting of norms for human relationships was exposed as it became apparent that many churches were holding out as the last bastion of white exclusivism. One side effect of that exposure was that the authority of the predominantly white churches as arbiters of normative standards was undermined. The credibility of the churches as keepers of the boundaries of good and righteous life lost ground in the public mind.

The revolt against tradition—spearheaded by black civil rights—was soon to be joined by other victims of perceived oppression from long-standing conventions in human relationships. The cruel and shabby treatment of native Americans by their white conquerors was brought into public view and the history of white European migration across the North American continent was rewritten to expose the injustice that cast a shadow across that history of the development of the western frontier. The frightened and unnecessary confinement of Japanese Americans in the "Jap-hating" days of the Pacific War came to light and was condemned as a blemish on the smooth face of America's image of itself as a nation of justice and goodwill.

Important as was the powerful movement of minority peoples into visibility in American society in the exposure of its history of injustice, it was not left to the minorities to carry the entire burden of demand for change. The exposure of the injustice and oppression previously hidden in the history of American society gathered increasing momentum as the dark underlay of paternalism and male dominance in the ancient patterns of androcentric Western culture began to be called into question. Women joined with other marginalized people to declare the injustice of the boundaries that set their traditional roles. As unjust restrictions on the creative use of women's talents and energies were confronted by increasing numbers of women, many of the most taken-for-granted boundaries that traditionally governed ordinary family and working life began to crumble. The most basic rules that governed relationships between the sexes began to change, more or less drastically, depending upon the degree of change in consciousness of individuals and couples.

Husbands who have for years assumed the authoritative leadership role in marriage and family life have suddenly been confronted by wives who are no longer content simply to be the help-mate who willingly provides the basics of care for home, husband, and children. Wives who had mother role models who asserted their influence on family decision making in covert ways, suddenly have become unwilling to "play that game" and have become more openly assertive toward sometimes puzzled husbands. Male pastors themselves have discovered that their

35

previously taken-for-granted use of masculine pronouns in the pulpit was no longer acceptable to a growing body of their female parishioners, including their own spouses!

On a level of perhaps no greater cultural significance, but one that confronted them with complex and thorny situations in their marriage and family counseling, pastors have found that they have been forced to deal with an increase in the incidence of severe marital conflict, sometimes ending in divorce, resulting from inabilities of marital partners to adapt to one or another aspect of the liberation of women from their traditional submissive or secondary role boundaries.

Martha and Joe Gibson were such a couple. In their mid-forties, the Gibsons had reared three bright and capable children. The oldest child, a daughter, had finished college, was engaged to an ambitious young man just out of law school. The middle child, a son, was in medical school and still financially and emotionally dependent on his parents. The youngest, also a son, was attending a prestigious private university at his parents' considerable expense.

Martha had always been an active woman whose club and church interests consumed as much of her considerable energy as did the task of providing a comfortable home for her husband and much nurturing attention for her children. Joe, a dentist with an active, but not over-busy practice, enjoyed golf, television, and reading. He was only minimally available to his wife as an emotional and conversational partner, preferring to be left to his own self-oriented interests. His concerns about his children had mostly to do with his worries about the mounting costs of their education, the expenses to be incurred by his daughter's impending marriage, and fears that his monetary and energy resources would be exhausted.

Having for several years been an enthusiastic participant in various efforts in her church to raise the consciousness of people concerning feminist perspectives on religious and social life, Martha was quite willing to seek employment outside the home as the school expenses of the children began to mount. With a full time job that challenged her, she still tried valiantly to do everything for home and children that she had always done. Meanwhile, her leadership abilities were receiving considerable recognition in her church, and there were yearly requests for her to serve in more and more responsible lay leadership posts. All of this activity, while entered into with great enthusiasm and energy, nevertheless had begun to take its toll on Martha's patient willingness to be the model help-mate at home. She became less and less tolerant of her husband's secluded unavailability and his complaints about money.

Joe, puzzled and covertly angered by her likewise increasingly angry demands that he become more of a participant in the marriage, withdrew further into himself.

The crisis came when Joe and Martha's pastor, unaware of the growing marital conflict, requested of Martha that she take on yet another major volunteer role in the church. On being informed about this request—a request Martha was quite unrealistically trying to rationalize accepting—Joe dug in his heels. The marital explosion that followed so strained the marital bonds that the pastor wisely referred Martha and Joe for marriage counseling. For months after that the Gibsons hovered on the verge of divorce. Fortunately, after several years of hard work in the counseling relationship and the necessarily slow process of greater development of independence on the part of the children, Martha and Joe have reached a new level of still tentative, but more hopeful, stability in their marriage. Their differences as persons still give them difficulty, but their acceptance of one another and of a more flexible model of marriage provides a workable basis for their continuing relationship.

Stories such as this one can, with individual variation, be told of countless conflicted marriages all across American society, beginning in the early seventies, continuing through the eighties, and still continuing into the nineties. To be sure, the conflicts in marriages that end in divorce have not all been caused by, or even necessarily related to, changes in consciousness on the part of women influenced by the feminist critique of marital icons. But there is ample evidence that this strong, and sometimes subtle, shift in consciousness has participated in loosening many of the traditional bonds that held American marriages together. Equally, there is ample evidence that the basic structure of American family life has shifted away from the patterns of patriarchy.

While taking nothing away from the powerful impact of the black civil rights movement for fundamental change in human relationship norms, it becomes increasingly clear as time goes on that the revisions in the cultural infrastructure beneath many of the foundational customs of Western social life being initiated by feminists are far more radical than those demanded by civil rights activists. Radical as the demand for civil liberties by blacks and other ethnic minorities seemed to their reactionary opponents, the fundamental basis for the plea for civil rights was to call American society back to its norms and vision for the new society as stated in the founding documents of the republic. Biblical legitimations proclaimed to undergird the demand for equality between the races were, in most respects, legitimations that had been verbally affirmed by the dominant white majority both within the churches and in the secular public realm.[10]

The feminist critique of American—indeed of all of Western cultural normative practices—is of a quite different order. Within that movement, not only have the long-affirmed social practices that set normative boundaries around the role expectations of the two sexes and the relationships between them been challenged, but also the very basis of the culture itself has been disputed at a more fundamental level. The androcentric and paternalistic biases of the classic texts on which the culture has over centuries been formed at every level have been uncovered and exposed as themselves embodying inequity and injustice toward women.[11]

The feminist theologian Catherine Keller builds her convincing theological critique of Western androcentrism on both her studies of Western myths, and the pervasive psychological history of grounding authentic selfhood in the necessity of "separation," "independence," and "autonomy": all, she says, are images derived from the masculine orientation of Western cultural history from its beginnings.

> Quite naturally, the human imitates its image of the divine. But quite unnaturally, antinaturally—with heroic artifice—the divine became the male alone. Human "heroes" imitate and incarnate divine ones, and soon even the matter of myth or of theology becomes irrelevant, unconscious, whether accepted or rejected. Then we cannot even wrestle with the assailants or the angels of the tradition. But the image keeps working with mythic force. Marduk's victory, Yahweh's triumph over the Deep, Perseus' confrontation by destruction of the Gorgon—these manifest the root-metaphor of heroic achievement. The defeat of the "female thing" eventuates in the paradigm of the radically separative self.[12]

In a somewhat more moderate manner, but with no less intention of critique and radical revision, the metaphorical theologian Sallie McFague asserts that the virtually exclusively male, patriarchal metaphors for God and the human-God relationship that dominate traditional Christian usage must now be supplemented with metaphors that come from feminine and non-patriarchal experiential sources. God as Mother, Friend, and Lover are images that not only complement the dominantly androcentric metaphors found in biblical and traditional Christian theological texts, but also, in McFague's view, are more nearly true to contemporary human experience.

> Christian theology, in our time at least, cannot be merely or mainly hermeneutics, that is, interpretation of the tradition, a translation of ancient

creeds and concepts to make them relevant for contemporary culture. Rather, theology must be self-consciously constructive, willing to think differently than in the past. . . . Theology in our day needs to be self-consciously constructive in order to free itself from traditional notions of divine sovereignty.[13]

Such notions embedded in the biblical tradition, McFague contends, need now to be supplemented—even countered—with a broad range of metaphorical images that counteract the dominance of fundamentally masculine and paternalistic metaphors in the historic texts of Christian tradition.

While the feminist critique of established religious tradition to which I have referred thus far has had its direct impact largely within theological and liturgical circles, its effort to break down the dominance of masculine boundaries has begun to evidence a much wider influence. Joined by feminists who develop their arguments not so much on religious or ethical grounds as on psychologically grounded assertion of the uniqueness of women's experience, these women have engaged in revisionist critique of such male-dominated psychological theories as the Freudian psychoanalytic tradition. While the empirical validation for her theories about the unique nature of female development remains incomplete, the argument made by such developmental psychologists as Carol Gilligan for the particularity of female as over against male development has been widely accepted.[14] The implicit norm of male patterns of individuation and achievement of autonomous independence is being strongly challenged by the assertion of the normative value of female patterns that emphasize relatedness and participation.

It can be argued that this form of feminist critique has only begun to penetrate to the level of popular culture within which the common people of the society live out the details of their lives and set boundaries on their behavior. Androcentricity and paternalism are still very alive in American popular culture! But an uneasiness with male dominance and a concomitant uneasiness with role boundaries that govern common patterning of family and work relationships are abroad in the land. The lines of authority between the sexes and between both male and female marital partners and their parents and children are much less clearly drawn. Increasing numbers of marriages and families seem to be living with unclear maps of the relational territory they encompass. Male dominance of the working world still—in many respects—appears secure, but numerous economic and social factors seem daily to shorten the life expectancy of the rule of men in the working place.

3. The resurgence of the religious right and popular reactions to it.

Readers who follow the flow of daily news reporting do not need to be reminded that this emerging popular thrust against the boundaries of male and paternal control of everyday life in American culture has encountered a strong counter-thrust: that of the so-called moral majority, or religious right. Taking advantage of the high visibility provided by television, the televangelists have mounted a formidable popular front that presses for "the return to old time values." More and more narrowly focused in the public mind on issues such as abortion, prayer in the public schools, homosexuality, and marital infidelity, this resurgence of cultural conservativism has served to rally and make politically active large numbers of religious fundamentalists to the cause of tightened restrictions on individual behavior and conservative religious control of public standards. Having moved into the public arena of politics and national affairs, leaders of this movement have, to a considerable extent, succeeded in conjoining their conservative ideology with regard to individual and family morality with pleas for a return to nationalistic, militaristic patriotism.

Not unexpectedly, this vocally clamorous cry to return to the religious conservatism of the past appears to have prompted its own less blatantly vocal, but nevertheless potent, counter-thrust from cultural liberals who argue for societal recognition of individual right of choice. The homosexual community has become more vocal and politically organized. Supporters of the right of free choice concerning abortion have become organized and assertive in the political and legal arenas. Opponents of prayer in the public schools have become politically active in some states. Even those most rebelliously libertarian practitioners of sexual freedom, the so-called "swingers," now have a national organization and hold conventions in the open arena of big city convention hotels. Further fragmentation of centrist consensual standards with regard to more and more issues of personal and corporate morality and day-to-day life practices is one of the results of this popular cultural battle. Yet another less publicly visible result is that for many persons, particularly among the educated classes in the cities, the churches' norm and boundary setting role—the role of envisioning the basics of American common life—has been further eroded, if not made irrelevant.

4. An increased popular awareness of the pluralism of cultures.

The contentious thrust and counterthrust of revisionism from within the dominant North American culture in recent years has taken place within an atmosphere of enormously greater awareness of the pluralism of world cultures. Now made much more recognizable to the average citizen because of things such as the mass media, the greatly increased presence in America of refugee peoples from all over the world, and increases in world travel and cultural exchange programs, recognition of pluralism in language, values, behavioral customs, and the like, is now commonplace. Although the visible presence of cultural diversity within and on the fringes of mainstream middle-class life is on occasion experienced as an unwanted interruption of the consensual flow of the way things are in America, to an increasing extent cultural diversity gives impetus to a new awareness of and affirmation concerning pluralism.

The influence of pluralism on American cultural life has shifted perceptibly during the period following World War II. Though America has for centuries prided itself on being the melting pot for peoples from other parts of the world, until the changes discussed earlier began, the common understanding was that those entering the American cultural scene should become "Americanized" as quickly as possible. Now the atmosphere of expectation has subtly shifted toward encouragement of so-called ethnic groups to keep their language and customs distinctively alive and in some degree of critical dialogue with standard American cultural practice. The pluralism of ways of life and the particularity of differing cultural histories has moved tenuously, but definitely, up on the scale of what is to be valued in American life. Otherness has increased in value. Sameness has, concomitantly, lost ground as a cultural standard. One of the equally subtle results of this shift in valuing of pluralism is that the dominant value, behavioral, and relational standards of the white middle class have been relativized.

It is just at this point that the more normatively critical perspectives represented by black, feminist, and other liberationist groups have been unselfconsciously appropriated by popular culture as legitimations for a much less disciplined loosening of the grip of traditional norms on everyday life. It is as if, having been challenged powerfully by the critiques of liberation, traditional boundaries of all kinds have become less secure in the popular mind, perhaps even suspect. The result is a more pervasive mood of uncertainty, questioning, and antinomianism in the affairs of everyday life.

THE ROLE OF TRADITION IN SETTING NORMS
AND BOUNDARIES

After reading what has been said concerning cultural revisionism and pluralism up to this point, the reader may think that the argument of this book will be to stand against or at least be strongly critical of what I have argued to be the causal factors beneath the current fragmentation of norms and visional boundaries in American life. Lest that be the mistaken impression, I must hasten to say that this is indeed not the case. I shall contend, quite to the contrary, that there is much to rejoice about in the yeasty ferment that pervades the American cultural scene in the latter decades of the twentieth century.

While the new search for norms and boundaries in the context of greater openness, even uncertainty, disagreement, and press for revision of cultural icons, is a sign of crisis, it is better seen as also being an indication of healthy ferment in a culture grown stale and stultifying. To say that is not to say that there is no danger in our present situation. Indeed, the possibilities that American culture can either fall into anarchy or revert to a pattern of heavy-handed conservative control are both possibilities that could become realities. But a time of interruption and openness to revision may also be a time of *kairos*, when something truly new and transforming may break upon the American cultural scene.

For the Christian pastor whose task it is to give leadership to a congregation of people as they individually and collectively find their way through the unmapped wilderness of a time of radical cultural change, the situation confronting us presents some complex and puzzling problems. As leader of a community whose very name roots it deeply in a particular narrative contained in its sacred texts, the pastor is called upon to represent that tradition faithfully and authoritatively. In certain important respects, the pastor is the embodiment of that tradition. The people called to be loyal to the Christian community and its tradition look to the pastor for interpretive guidance with primary attention being given to the faithful representation of that tradition. To carry out that interpretive task, the pastor must thus be both an interpreter of the sacred texts of the tradition and an interpreter of the signs of the times. Bringing these two interpretive responsibilities into some meaningful and pertinent dialogical relationship is central to the role of the pastor. As I have argued in my earlier book, *Widening the Horizons: Pastoral Responses to a Fragmented Society*, it is the role that gives coherence to all the various functions of parish ministry.[15]

Fulfilling the interpretive guidance task, particularly as it relates to the interpretation of questions concerning norms and boundaries, presents peculiar and difficult problems for the pastor who has been sensitized to the signs of the times to which I have pointed earlier. That is the case not only because the image of the pastor as representative of a tradition has been implanted in the minds of ordinary people in particular and sometimes distorted ways, but also because several of the cultural thrusts for change have been critical of traditional modes of thinking concerning norms and boundaries. To be perceived as a primary representative of a tradition at a time when that tradition is under fire from some as having fostered oppression, and from others as having been interpreted in too "liberal" or "unbiblical" a fashion, is to find oneself in an uncomfortable position. The path of faithful interpretation of the tradition that is also supportive of a truly new search for norms is indeed narrow and fraught with many possibilities for stumbling!

It is just at this point that a certain clarity of thought about what it means to "live in" and represent a tradition becomes most essential. For many, particularly among the younger generations, the popular image associated with that phrase tends to be strongly colored with the meanings of metaphors such as old-fashioned, dated, and closed, as opposed to up-to-date, contemporary, and open. For others who consider themselves to be of a more conservative mindset, the metaphors that surround that phrase will more likely be loyalty, time-tested, and preservation of traditional values. To live in and represent a tradition are thus seen by many in popular culture as to be constrained, bound, perhaps even hampered by the past. For others, its meaning connotes loyalty to popular interpretations of the tradition of the relatively recent past. Apt to have representatives of both extremes of these contradictory metaphorical meanings of tradition in her or his parish, the pastor may frequently feel caught in the middle.

The more precise meaning of tradition as that concept has been developed by hermeneutical philosophers is in sharp contrast with these popular appropriations of the term. For such philosophers as Hans-Georg Gadamer, a noted German scholar of the interpretation of historical texts and other human artifacts, to live in a tradition is not something one chooses to do or not do. In fundamental ways, humans who live in a culture are constituted by that culture's tradition. One is therefore not so much an interpreter of a tradition as one is oneself interpreted by a tradition. This is to say that, most often in ways that we are only dimly aware of, we who have grown up and been nurtured in the culture formed by the Judeo-Christian tradition of the West have had our ways of perceiving, ordering, and evaluating experiences of the world shaped by that tradition. Even the most avant-garde advocate of change cannot escape the influence of tradition. The very issues upon which such persons make their plea for change will have been shaped by that tradition's way of seeing and comprehending the world.

Tradition, for Gadamer, is not a static, unchanging entity. Rather, it is a historical process that moves and develops in time.

The historical movement of human life consists in the fact that it is never utterly bound to any one standpoint, and hence can never have a truly closed horizon. The horizon is, rather, something into which we move and that moves with us. Horizons change for a person who is moving. Thus the horizon of the past, out of which all human life lives and which exists in the form of tradition, is always in motion. It is not historical consciousness that first sets the surrounding horizon in motion. But in it this motion becomes aware of itself.[16]

Thus, for Gadamer, to be faithful in one's representation of the horizon of the Christian tradition does not mean to be bound to or hemmed in by the mode of interpretation of that tradition that took place in any historical time period, be that the time of the originators of the sacred texts of the tradition or the time of the Reformers, or any other historical period. Rather, to be faithful to that tradition is to bring the preunderstandings (prejudices is Gadamer's word, though it must be remembered that he uses that term in a non-pejorative sense) of that tradition into dialogue with the realities of life in the present time. The horizon formed by those preunderstandings is to be put at risk as we enter into the varying horizons of contemporary life recognizing their otherness from our tradition-shaped horizon, and allowing those other horizons to speak to us, raise their questions for us, and offer their alternative ways of seeing the world to us. Faithful interpretation of one's tradition thus involves tending the historical process of its development. The tradition's horizon in its interplay with the otherness of an emerging horizon shaped by changing historical circumstances fuses with that otherness to form a reinterpretation of the meaning and mandates of one's tradition, now reconsidered. The historical process of an ongoing, living tradition has thus been nurtured and tended both faithfully and in the spirit of innovation.

If we are to take seriously this living, historical, process-oriented understanding of what it means to live in and represent a tradition, we will attend carefully to the ever-changing shape of contemporary life while yet retaining a strong anchor in the sacred texts of the Christian tradition. We will watch and listen for ways in which the emerging cultural issues of our time interrupt our accustomed ways of interpreting Christianity's sacred texts. These interruptions may cause us to interpret again and anew the core meanings of those texts. We may discover that there are aspects of the sacred texts that we have heretofore overlooked or so taken for granted that the force of their meaning has been covered over, their implications for contemporary life left untended.

Such reinterpretations of biblical narrative texts as those presented by the feminist biblical scholar Phyllis Trible are excellent examples of the way in which emerging issues in contemporary society can prompt a renewed search of the scriptural sources of a tradition in ways that interrupt long-standing habitual modes of interpretation. In the Introduction to her powerfully prophetic book, *Texts of Terror*, she writes:

> As a critique of culture and faith in light of misogyny, feminism is a prophetic movement, examining the status quo, pronouncing judgment, and calling for repentance. This hermeneutic engages scripture in various ways. One approach documents the case against women. It cites and evaluates long neglected data that show the inferiority, subordination, and abuse of the female in ancient Israel and the early church. By contrast, a second approach discerns within the Bible critiques of patriarchy. It upholds forgotten texts and reinterprets familiar ones to shape a remnant theology that challenges the sexism of scripture. Yet a third approach incorporates the other two. It recounts tales of terror *in memoriam* to offer sympathetic readings of abused women. If the first perspective documents misogyny historically and sociologically, this one appropriates the data poetically and theologically. At the same time, it continues to search for the remnant in unlikely places.... In telling sad stories, a feminist hermeneutic seeks to redeem the time.[17]

Phyllis Trible not only points to ways in which the emerging insights and issues of the present time can and indeed should force a careful reexamination of the sacred texts of the Christian tradition, but also expresses in a most positive way the intentionality behind such efforts at reinterpretation. It is an effort to "redeem the time."

For ministry practitioners who have been sensitized to the deeper dimensions of the new search for norms and boundaries in contemporary Western culture, Trible's statement of the intention of feminist critique provides a model to be emulated. Rather than being "blown about by every chance wind of doctrine" that besets a time of cultural transition, the practitioner is called to join in the effort to reexamine the sacred texts that have shaped the Christian community. Following the example of such persons as Phyllis Trible, the minister is called upon to search deeply and imaginatively into the treasure-trove of biblical stories and accounts of the origins of our tradition in search of images and metaphorical themes that, when brought into dialogue with our present cultural confusion, can assist us in relocating ourselves. For us, the relocation of boundaries and the renewed effort to shape norms for living is not one to be undertaken simply on an ad hoc, strictly here-and-now basis. Rather, as laypersons and leaders of a faithful community responsible for the tending of our community's historical process, we will look once more to the texts of our sacred origins for metaphorical guidance, looking now with eyes that have seen the signs of the times in which we find ourselves.

THE SEARCH OF THE TRADITION IN PASTORAL THEOLOGY

The present time in the historical development of pastoral care and counseling as a discipline of ministry is a time marked by a groundswell of interest in reconsidering the primary theoretical basis on which pastoral work has been done during the so-called modern period of pastoral care (roughly speaking, the last fifty years). Confronted both with what some see as the virtual hegemony of psychological language and ways of thinking in the field of pastoral care *and* the increasing fragmentation of a heavily psychologized cultural context, some—though not by any means all—of the leaders of the pastoral care movement have turned their thinking in a theological direction. One result of that renewed interest in recovery of theological origins in relation to pastoral work is that a number of somewhat varying proposals have been presented as ways by which that reorientation of the field might take place. This book, when seen in sequence with my last two books, *The Living Human Document* and *Widening the Horizons*, extends my effort to contribute to that corporately undertaken task by giving specific attention to the issue of reformulating the Christian community's sense of location concerning norms, boundaries, and visions of the good life. The mode of inquiry here presented is, therefore, the mode of a narrative, hermeneutical, pastoral theology.

As was the case with my earlier books, the interest that drives the writing of this book is a very practical one. As I have reflected on my own work as a teacher of pastoral care and practitioner of pastoral counseling, and as I have listened to pastors talk about their deeper concerns in their ministerial work, I am struck with the number and complexity of human problems we pastors are encountering that involve confusion and conflict over norms, boundaries, and visions of what life should be. Why is this the case? What is happening in the common life of our people that is fostering such confusion, such polarizing of the common opinions of people not only about morals and values, but also about a fundamental, structuring vision of human relationships in families and communities? What can and should pastors be doing in their everyday work of pastoral ministry to respond to this situation of boundary confusion?

To answer these questions requires getting beneath the surface of the problems as they are presented to us in particular situations. It requires asking questions about the culture that shapes our common life. It also requires careful reflection on specific situations in which these normative problems appear in order that the concrete phenomena present in those situations can speak for themselves. Furthermore, if the perspective from which we are to respond pastorally to these situations is to be a pastoral *theological* perspective, it will require careful probing of the theological

46

grounding that authorizes the approach to be taken. As the plots of many modern novels seem to require, there are several threads or sub-plots yet to be developed before the full thrust of the tack I am proposing can be fleshed out.

In this chapter, we have sought to dig beneath one aspect of the fragmentation of Western culture, that of cultural norms and visional boundaries, in search of a number of its socio-historical process roots. We have also begun the work of opening up the potentially promising possibilities to be found in hermeneutical dialogue between a fresh search of the sacred texts of Christian origins and contemporary experiences of fragmentation. As I proposed in *Widening the Horizons*, it is through the fusion of horizons made possible by such dialogue that a transformation of our understanding of our situation and the way ahead out of that situation may be found.[18]

I turn in chapter 2 toward the practical task the parish pastor (or layperson) confronts when seeking to understand a situation that arises in the everyday life of a community involving issues related to norms and visional boundaries. Utilizing one such situation that occurred in a white, middle-class neighborhood as a prototypical situation of sorts, my intention will be to inquire into how ordinary people in a community make their normative boundary decisions. The specific situation has to do with a controversy concerning control of physical boundaries and the intrusion of outsiders into those boundaries. When seen in metaphorical meaning terms, however, the controversy over physical boundaries takes on broader, deeper meaning dimensions. The notion I want to pursue is that in the course of our common life we make most decisions by the exercise of what we call common sense. Drawing upon a somewhat neglected aspect of the philosophical hermeneutics tradition, the aesthetic hermeneutics of Hans-Georg Gadamer, chapter 2 will attempt to break open what we mean by common sense, explore some of the ways common sense itself is shaped historically, and propose ways in which common sense can exercise either oppressive or transformative power in relation to norms and boundaries. Chapter 2 envisions ways in which the work of the pastor can enable transformations in the common sense understanding of God's people. If persons do in fact tend to make their normative decisions by the use of their common sense, then it follows that in our ministry to persons in situations in which normative issues are at stake, it is upon common sense that ministry must have its impact.

CHAPTER TWO

BY REASON OR
BY THE IMAGINATION?

Common Sense and the Normative in Everyday Life

Reflection on the task of the pastoral care practitioner in relation to the loss of boundaries, norms, and visions in contemporary life does not have to penetrate very deeply beneath the surface of the problem before encountering the complex question concerning how ordinary people make their decisions when confronted with boundary questions. As one earnest but frustrated young pastor expressed it, "They sure don't make their ethical choices like we were taught to make them in Ethics 101!"

BOUNDARY ISSUES IN DAY-TO-DAY LIVING

The frustration this pastor was experiencing may be seen as a direct by-product of the contextual location within which the pastor ministers. It is the context of the flow of ordinary life, whether that be the ordinary life of a white middle-class suburban church and its community, or the very different flow of everyday experience in an inner-city ghetto, or a town-and-country farming community. Though each of these contexts will reflect the larger cultural patterns of thought that dominate a given part of the world, they will also evidence a more diversified particularity, depending upon the socio-cultural location of the congregation and its community. They will likewise reflect the flux and change of fragmented cultural transformations, some of which I have sketched out in the previous chapter. In any case, the pastor is always in the situation of having to represent her or his understanding of the claims and normative expectations of Christian existence within the contextual ebb and flow of the ordinary life of a people. To fulfill that representative, interpretive role means that the pastor must frequently act as go-between or translator in an often confused and confusing conversation among fundamentally different ways of talking about where the boundaries for living ought to be.

The task this chapter undertakes is to see if some conceptual and observational tools may be found that may assist the pastor in coming to grips with the problem my young pastor friend pointed to so forcefully. How do ordinary people, generally unschooled in the ways of logical, carefully reasoned ethical reflection, make their day-to-day choices with regard to boundaries and norms? Is there a hidden logic inherent in that process—a logic that Don Browning in his book, *Religious Ethics and Pastoral Care*, speaks of as "practical moral reasoning"?[1] Or do these decisions tend more often to be made more intuitively, in the manner of living out some imagined story of how life is or should be? Is the process of everyday normative judgment-making a process governed more by reason or by the imagination? This is the issue I want to address in this chapter, preliminary to taking up the issue of pastoral care of persons experiencing boundary difficulties concerning how the good life is to be envisioned.

Our approach to this preliminary problem will be first to examine an example of a community in process of making a decision about boundaries. Reflection on that concrete situation will prompt us to take a hermeneutical detour of sorts into several theoretical frameworks, hoping that they may illuminate the situation in helpful ways. Specifically, the approach being taken in this book will require that we delve into a portion of the literature of hermeneutical phenomenology in search of some general observations concerning how cultural traditions tend to function to establish and maintain certain ways of seeing the world and envisioning the good and appropriate life in the world. With that set of observations in mind, we will then return to the case example and thereby test the observational tools we have collected and see if they open a way toward further reflection on the pastoral task in our contemporary cultural situation of boundary fragmentation.

BY REASON OR BY THE IMAGINATION: A COMMONPLACE EXAMPLE OF THE PROBLEM

My example occurred in a very ordinary and relatively stable middle-class neighborhood located in the inner ring of suburbs of a large metropolitan community. I choose to use it because it is a clear example of a community in process of quite literally and physically making a boundary decision. It is, however, a boundary decision with wider and more profoundly significant normative cultural implications for that community. The geographical boundary decision, therefore, may serve as a metaphor for seeing how a community corporately exercises its normative visional function.

The neighborhood in question is located near one of its county's busy, recently become bi-racial high schools. Every fall when school begins, persons living in that neighborhood have observed with some variation a similar set of occurrences. High school students in increasing numbers drive their own automobiles to school. They come down the neighborhood streets at speeds that considerably exceed the speed limits posted on the street. Furthermore, recently it has been observed by residents that the number of cars has so increased that parking has become a serious problem. The small parking lot at the high school, even when supplemented part of the time by the spaces in a church parking lot adjacent to the school, is unable to hold all the cars. So the young people park in front of houses along the street wherever they can find a place and for a block or two away from the school all available space in front of homes is jammed with cars of all ages, models, and descriptions.

Recently, about a month into a new school year, a small group of parents who live near the school started a drive to get signatures of residents on a petition to be presented to the county government demanding that parking on the street be prohibited from 8:00 A.M. to 4:00 P.M. Monday through Friday. Accordingly, so the story told by one couple living in the neighborhood goes, one evening a young mother of several small children came to their door asking for signatures. She spoke of her and her neighbors' desire to restore the street to the uncluttered tranquility the residents enjoyed during the summer. She spoke of her concern for the safety of the little children on the street. According to the story, the housewife who answered the doorbell, a mature woman in her sixties who had, with her husband, reared several children, all of whom were grown, pointed to her little old Honda parked in front of the house, saying that her car was always parked there. Furthermore, she noted her neighbor Norma's car across the street and the next door neighbor Carl's truck that stood much of the time in front of their house. "Ours is a busy neighborhood with lots of cars and small driveways. I can't ask all these people not to park in front of their own houses all day long, and I surely don't want to have to crowd our two cars on the driveway all the time. Furthermore, the high

50

school kids need to park somewhere. Many of them are now driving some distance in order to take advantage of the minority to majority transfer system and get to a better school than the one in their own neighborhood. Lots of those young people have to drive to after school jobs. What about them?"

Needless to say, neither of the resident members of the reporting household signed the petition. However, a majority of the residents of the neighborhood did sign, and the signs forbidding parking on the street during school hours subsequently appeared. A community has reaffirmed its boundaries and, at least insofar as parking on the street is concerned, "outsiders" have been excluded. The tranquility of a white, middle-class neighborhood has, at least to a degree, been restored.

What is going on in this little conflict of boundaries in an ordinary middle-class neighborhood? Decisions about norms and boundaries are certainly being made. But how? How are these ordinary people going about it?

Let us first look closely at the conversation between the two women. Is there anything we can see going on in that conversation that might be seen as "practical moral reasoning"? Clearly there is, both in the young mother's expression of concern for her and her neighbor's children, and in the older woman's talk about her and her neighbors' cars—and even more so in her references to the black young people who must drive to a better school and to work.

First, however, I want to propose that beneath and prior to the evident moral or even practical reasoning process taking place, there are two more fundamental and intuitive processes at work that are shaping the direction of decision. The first of these processes is imagistic in its basic structure, and at the level of deep recall of primary stories that have shaped those images of life in a neighborhood community. Those primary stories have shaped what might be called a certain aesthetic vision of what a neighborhood is and should be for the participants in that community. For some, hovering in the background are memories of quiet streets and uncluttered life among people one knows and cares about. For one of the participants in this neighborhood incident, the strange cars are an intrusion into that tranquil story. For the other participant, the threat of a petition to set tight boundaries is an intrusion on taken-for-granted structures of understanding concerning neighbors and their necessary actions in parking their cars in front of their homes. There are also conflicting narratives concerning who is to be considered one's neighbor with accompanying rights and privileges to be included within the

51

boundaries to be set for community life. The ancient story that responds to the question, "Who is my neighbor?" hovers quietly in the background. It speaks softly, imagistically of primary norms for neighborliness.

A second process at work is relational in very primal and down-to-earth ways. The young woman circulating the petition was doing so out of concern for a certain relationship that for her is primary, namely her relationship to her young children who play in the front yards of her and her immediate neighbors' homes. She seeks to protect those children by the exclusion of the intruders. The other woman's response to the petition request, on the other hand, suggests that the request for her signature on the petition not only impinges on her own needs (she parks her car in the street), but also impinges on a set of relational ties not only to her immediate neighbors, but also, at least in her imagination, to the young people who either venture out of their own neighborhoods in search of a better school, or must drive to school because they have jobs to get to when school is over. Those imagined relational ties undoubtedly have some origins in the semi-retired woman's earlier life experience as a mother of a large family, several of whom had to drive their cars to work before and after school. For her, the immediate relational ties to close neighbors are thus extended to a wider circle of anonymous persons who, as they live in her imagination, have legitimate needs that bring them to school in their cars that clutter the neighborhood streets.

The recognition that this ordinary incident in an urban neighborhood contains a conflict of images concerning the meaning of neighbor and neighborhood brings immediately to our awareness the fact that the incident reenacts an old conflict with deep roots in the human story. The question concerning who one's neighbor is has shaped the plot of many a human story across the centuries. It is a central feature of the plot of the biblical story of the stresses and strains of human relationships. Furthermore, the plot of this small vignette of differences of vision concerning neighborliness reveals the presence of another narrative theme that has taken root in American life—the theme of privatization. "My street is the private domain of me and my neighbors. That private domain must be protected. It must be guarded from invasion by outsiders and involvement in the public issues of the day as those issues are present in the public schools." The image of neighbor with roots in the biblical texts concerning neighborliness is brought into conflict with the images of that other American story that divides life into the public and the private sphere. One might even suggest that the conflict in the story can be seen as a conflict over whether the street that gives access to the homes in the neighborhood is public or private space.[2]

Although I can make no claim to having researched it empirically, I would hazard a guess that of the 95 percent of the people in the neighborhood who signed the petition, very few will have thought about any connection between the issue of setting tight boundaries on parking on the street to keep out the outsiders and the biblical query concerning who is one's neighbor. Rather, the warm image of a friendly and private neighborhood street and whatever is left of the biblical image of loving one's neighbors have become so fused in their minds as to be virtually identical. To the degree that that is the case, the biblical image of neighbor may be seen as a lost or dead image. As the German political theologian Johann Baptist Metz would put it, it is now a "dangerous memory."[3] And to press the political, liberationist theological language just a bit farther, the intrusion of the teenagers and their cars comes as an interruption, a break in the fabric of a taken-for-granted, story-shaped world. The interruption must therefore be resisted, and the dangerous memory suppressed.

The pastor with sensitive ears and eyes who moves into a new situation will soon learn that in that community, certain things are taken for granted as normative. They are the things that seemingly everyone in the community knows are either within or outside the boundaries of acceptable thought and behavior. Even those who may occasionally or habitually violate those norms know that they have stepped outside the limits of ordinary life in that community. Common sense tells everyone that that is the case. Common-sense wisdom also acknowledges that there are other aspects of human interaction and behavior that are, in that community, subject to individual choice and idiosyncratic perspective. Cheating on one's spouse or stealing from one's employer will, most often, by common consensus be understood to lie well outside the accepted norms of the community. Even with such actions as these, however, the pastor may find that in certain contexts those boundaries have become somewhat blurred by the equally common sense or consensual notion that "everyone is doing it."

With regard to some matters such as relationships between the races or appropriate sexual role boundaries, there may be rather sharp disagreements within a given community concerning what common sense norms dictate. Thus a certain subgroup, or even individual particularity, begins to introduce itself into the notion of what by common sense is believed to be true or appropriate. A certain "fellowship of kindred minds" is developed that confirms for members of the subgroup a particular judgment on a controversial matter. Thus a common sense or common mind is preserved by the subgroup.

THE SHAPING OF COMMON SENSE BY CULTURAL TRADITIONS

In ordinary usage then, the term *common sense* refers to a commonly held understanding of the way life is or should be. As the hermeneutical philosopher Hans-Georg Gadamer says in his account of how traditions shape and perpetuate ways of life:

> Common sense is seen primarily in the judgments about right and wrong, proper and improper, that it makes. Whosoever has a sound judgment is not thereby enabled to judge particulars under universal viewpoints, but he [or she] knows what is important, i.e., he [or she] sees things from right and sound points of view.[4]

Gadamer lifts up two ideas that are fundamental to understanding the way commonly held cultural notions of boundaries and norms operate in a community. He says they are *not* based upon the ability to "judge particulars under universal viewpoints." That is to say, they are not necessarily based upon some carefully constructed logic grounded in universal principles of ethics and values. One does not achieve the reputation of having common sense by demonstrated intellectual argumentation. Rather, to have common sense is simply to evidence "right and sound points of view" from within that particular cultural context. One simply knows what is right and what is wrong, and what is proper and what is improper, within that cultural tradition.

In the section of Gadamer's *Truth and Method* from which I have quoted, Gadamer is delving into the history of Western culture and seeking to uncover the ways in which the understandings of truth and normativity have been greatly influenced by aesthetics—the sense of what is true because it is beautiful. Exercising the care in attention to historical detail that is characteristic of German philosophers and theologians, Gadamer unpacks that history to show that in the development of what he refers to as Western humanistic culture, truth, beauty, and morality have been closely intertwined. To be a person with good taste in regard to beauty has meant to be closer to the truth than one without taste. And, as Gadamer says Immanuel Kant was able to show, "the idea of taste was originally more a moral than an aesthetic idea."[5]

> Thus it is primarily a question of taste not only to recognise this or that as beautiful, but to have an eye to the whole, with which everything that is beautiful must harmonise. Thus taste is not a community sense, in that it is dependent on an empirical universality, the complete unanimity of the judgments of others. It does not say that everyone will agree with our judgment, but that they should agree with it. . . . Against the tyranny

exercised by fashion, sure taste preserves a specific freedom and superiority. This is its real normative power, which is peculiar to it alone, the knowledge that it is certain of the agreement of an ideal community. In contrast to the ruling of taste by fashion, we see here the ideality of good taste. It follows that taste makes an act of knowledge—in a manner, it is true, which cannot be separated from the concrete situation on which it operates and cannot be reduced to rules and concepts.[6]

In an imaginatively provocative book about how skilled practitioners across a wide range of disciplines think about concrete problems in their practical work, Massachusetts Institute of Technology professor Donald A. Schon proposes that all reflective practice of a profession involves construal of the problem at hand within some theoretical frame of reference that at first glance may appear to be more or less remote from the problem at issue. Such theoretical frameworks can, says Schon, so reframe the problem in ways that open the possibility of new and creative solutions.[7] In the spirit of Schon's understanding of how theoretical frameworks can serve to open old problems to new solutions, I am here proposing that Gadamer's analysis of aesthetic hermeneutics, including his development of the concepts of common sense, sound judgment, and good taste, may indeed offer a potentially fruitful avenue of reflection that is worth pursuing concerning such commonplace dilemmas as the street parking problem.

Let us assume for the moment that it is true, as my frustrated young student pastor thought he had discovered, that ordinary people, in making their decisions about norms and boundaries, most of the time do not engage in careful and logical ethical reasoning. Rather, they most often trust in the wisdom of their common sense. In doing so, they may follow what Gadamer has found historically in Western culture to be thought of as the exercise of good taste, whatever that may be considered to be in their particular cultural context. To the extent that this is the case, our effort to uncover how ordinary people make their boundary decisions will necessitate uncovering the sources of common sense and good taste in communities. How do people come to know what makes common sense and what is good taste in their socio-cultural world?

In his usage of the three key concepts of common sense, sound judgment, and good taste in his aesthetic hermeneutics, Gadamer makes use of both attention to what is commonly understood as good and true by a cultural community, and recognition of a normativity that transcends commonly held ideals. Persons recognized as capable of exercising sound judgment and/or good taste thus both represent the cultural ethos and transcend it or set a normative standard for it. Their transcendent perspective is rooted in their richer, deeper, more accurate appropriation of the deepest narrative structures of their tradition, and in their greater capacity to relate the incident-bound parts of a community's activities to the whole of their aesthetic vision of what life in that community should be.

I would suggest that our inquiry into how ordinary persons make their boundary decisions—in just such situations as that in the neighborhood with the parking controversy—can be greatly illuminated by bringing to bear Gadamer's explication of the notions of common sense, sound judgment, and aesthetic taste as related to moral truth as a framework of reflection on the problem. By itself, that approach may not prove adequate. We will perhaps need additional conceptual tools to further achieve an adequate understanding of the processes by which common sense and good taste come to mean certain things in a given community. That problem will be taken up in a subsequent section of this chapter as we move to consider the theological ethical perspective of H. Richard Niebuhr. Before leaving Gadamer's history of aesthetics and taste, however, there is one further idea significant enough to take with us; namely, the idea that aesthetic judgment has traditionally included an understanding of what is "fitting." That sense of what is fitting for a given situation emerges from a commonly held cultural vision of the whole of reality. Furthermore, the parts of that situation, if they are to embody truth, must fit with the whole of the situation at it is aesthetically envisioned.[8]

THE FITTING RESPONSE AND AN ETHIC OF RESPONSIBILITY

Gadamer's observation concerning "the fitting" will perhaps resonate as familiar to those who have read and incorporated H. Richard Niebuhr's *The Responsible Self* into their own thinking. Niebuhr develops his understanding of human responsibility as the fitting response of persons to circumstances and actions of others with which they are confronted.

> We may say that purposiveness seeks to answer the question: "What shall I do?" by raising as prior the question: "What is my goal, ideal, or telos?" Deontology tries to answer the moral query by asking, first of all: "What is the law and what is the first law of my life?" Responsibility, however, proceeds in every moment of decision and choice to inquire: "What is going on?" If we use value terms then the differences among the three approaches may be indicated by the terms, the *good,* the *right,* and the *fitting;* for teleology is

concerned always with the highest good to which it subordinates the right; consistent deontology is concerned with the right, no matter what may happen to our goods; but for the ethics of responsibility the *fitting* action, the one that fits into a total interaction as response and as anticipation of further response, is alone conducive to the good and alone is right.[9]

Unlike Gadamer, Niebuhr does not use the language of aesthetics in developing his concept of responsibility as fitting response. Rather, he grounds his ethic of the fitting action in the Reformed tradition of the three uses of the law stemming from Martin Luther and, more particularly, John Calvin. It was Calvin who emphasized the "third use of the law," namely, that of guidance of faithful people in the paths of virtuous living.[10] The fitting response of responsible persons is, for Niebuhr, dependent upon both a process of interpretation of what is going on in any particular human situation and upon an interpretation of the fitting response to what is going on as guided by an interpretation of the long history of religion and value as found in the Christian tradition. Concerning this latter element in the fitting response, Niebuhr says:

> The great religions in general, and Christianity in particular, make their not least significant attack on this universal human ethos by challenging our ultimate historical myth. They do present new laws; they do present to us new ideals. But beyond all this they make their impact on us by calling into question our whole conception of what is fitting—that is, of what really fits in—by questioning our picture of the context into which we now fit our actions.[11]

For Niebuhr, the ultimate—and therefore appropriate—context for evaluating all human actions is the context of the actions of God in creation and history. All humanly constructed contexts or construals of the context within which any event takes place are to be evaluated and made finally meaningful by their fit within that ultimate context. Anything less than that will be partial and subject to human distortion; it will in the end prove idolatrous.

If we bring into dialogical relationship the aesthetic understanding of the fitting taken from Gadamer and the Christian theological/ethical understanding of that concept as developed by Niebuhr, the fusion of those two horizons begins to shape a vision of the Christian understanding of the wisdom by which common sense is to be critically evaluated, and appropriately tasteful guidance provided. In carrying forward that dialogical fusion of horizons, it is important to keep in mind that Niebuhr, like Gadamer, is not speaking of a simple process of wooden obedience to tradition, but rather is embracing a continuous process of interpretation and reinterpretation of tradition. As a matter of fact, Niebuhr specifically rejects the interpretations of many Old Testament scholars who identify the ethic of the Israelite and early Christian communities as an ethic of obedience. Niebuhr sees instead the great prophetic and apostolic figures of the Bible exercising sound, responsible judgment in response to their interpretations of what is going on in the situations in which they found themselves.

> If now we approach the Scriptures with the idea of responsibility we shall find, I think, that the particular character of this ethics can be more fully if not wholly adequately interpreted. At the critical junctures in the history of Israel and of the early Christian community the decisive question [people] raised was not "What is the goal?" nor yet, "What is the law?" but "What is happening?" and then "What is the fitting response to what is happening?"[12]

Thus, it might be said that Niebuhr sees the prophetic and apostolic figures of the Bible as persons who, in the midst of the critical situations in which they found themselves, exercised, in Gadamer's terms, a certain good taste or sound judgment as to what was going on at the time and what a fitting response to what was going on might be. And, as Niebuhr sees it, that sense of the fitting was always linked to a commonly held understanding that God was active in the situation at hand—most particularly active in the actions of others upon those seeking to act responsibly.[13]

NARRATIVE SOURCES OF THE COMMON SENSE OF WHAT IS FITTING

Readers familiar with my earlier work will already have become acquainted with the narrative, hermeneutical approach to doing practical theological thinking that I developed in two books: *The Living Human Document: Re-Visioning Pastoral Counseling in a Hermeneutical Mode*[14] and *Widening the Horizons: Pastoral Responses to a Fragmented Society*.[15] In *The Living Human Document*, I proposed that the individual self, out of its individual and familial experience, its appropriation of the interpretations of faith and culture to which it has been exposed, and interpretations of its unique social situation beginning at a very early age, forms a more or less firm, more or less clearly articulated, mythic narrative of itself and of the world. Tending, maintaining, and reinterpreting that story is the central activity that makes up what I spoke of in that book as "the life of the soul."[16]

In *Widening the Horizons*, I further developed the narrative hermeneutical approach to practical theological thinking both by broadening the focal context under consideration to the communal, societal, and cultural levels, and by deepening and extending the biblical narrative theological basis that undergirds the task of narrative, hermeneutical practical theology.[17] Building upon the hermeneutical phenomenology of the human appropriation of time as formulated by Paul Ricoeur[18] and the concept of the fusion of horizons taken from Gadamer, I proposed that, when seen from a hermeneutical perspective, the central purpose of ministry practice is best fulfilled in assisting individuals, families, and communities in the transformation of life by means of the transformation and reinterpretation of their core stories. Such transformations, if they are to be seen as taking place within the ongoing Christian community and its tradition, should rightly be grounded in dialogical interaction with the primary images and themes of the biblical and Christian story of the Creator God and God's human family, the people of God.

Consistent with the narrative, hermeneutical stance of these two earlier books, I would here propose that beneath the content of all notions of common sense, sound judgment, and aesthetic taste—in the sense that Gadamer uses these concepts—lie the images, themes, evaluative suppositions, and ideal understandings of a commonly held story or complex of stories that have shaped that community and its tradition. To share in the common sense of that community is to have had one's own mythic life story shaped to fit the images, themes, evaluations, and ideals of the communal story. To exercise sound judgment in that community is to embody the normative images, themes, evaluations, and ideals found in the communal story. To be a person of good taste in that community is to express in one's life and behavior the aesthetic vision contained in the deepest images and metaphors of that communal story. Whether or not one sees oneself or is seen by others as possessing common sense, sound judgment, or good taste will depend upon the extent to which one's sense of things, one's judgment about things, and/or one's aesthetic taste concerning things matches those narratively grounded, commonly held notions. What is fitting in any given set of circumstances is therefore finally dependent upon what fits with the core story being lived out by the individual or the community under consideration.

It is important to acknowledge that one of the presuppositions contained in this narrative, hermeneutical perspective on the way communities form their narratives and maintain their traditions is that the ongoing, intergenerational life of any community is sustained over time by means of a dialectical interaction between events and human construction of interpretations of those events. The story of any community thus always involves a peculiar mixture of historical facts (events that occurred in their actuality) and imaginative fictions (human attachments of meaning to the events). Stories give accounts of events, but they are accounts of events that express the meaning of those events within the ongoing life of an individual or a community.[19]

It is just at this point that we encounter a fundamental problem for ministry that is a reflection of one of the most basic of all problems of human finitude. This is the problem that Ricoeur consistently refers to in his study of time and narrative as the *aporia* (impassable barrier) encountered in any effort finally to resolve the conflicts inherent in the interplay of events in time (facticity) and human narratives concerning those events (fictions).[20] Events in time and human interpretations of events interact in multifarious and subtle ways to shape and channel individual and corporate life in certain directions not fully under the control of the individual or the community. Both individual and corporate consciousness, including consciousness concerning what expresses common sense, sound judgment, and good taste is subject to the forceful flow of events, as well as the ebb and flow of interpretive meanings that cause events to be experienced in certain ways. This is what it means to be a finite human being or a finite human community.

The people of the Hebrew Bible, for example, had their consciousness of themselves forcefully shaped by the events of the Exodus. Those events made them the people of Exodus in ways they have never escaped or forgotten. But they became a people likewise shaped by the meaning-filled stories they attached to those events. Event and narrative meaning interacted to give a people a history and a communal consciousness of who they were. Any effort to separate out the power of the Exodus events from the storied meanings linked to those events would encounter, says Ricoeur, an impassable barrier.

Within this frame of reference, the words *tradition* and *traditional* do not simply refer to the way the world was seen and human activities structured a long time ago. Traditions are not simply the icons of a dead past. Rather, traditions are seen as living, dynamic, historical processes that move and change in the interaction between events and meanings over time, while remaining rooted in the primal images and metaphors of their historic beginnings. What Paul Ricoeur speaks of as traces of these deep roots of a tradition remain, often in subtle and hidden ways, in the life of a people embedded in that tradition. That is true even though persons reared in that tradition are living in circumstances very different from those of their progenitors.[21]

The forces of events and the meanings a tradition carries in its stories interact to both limit human freedom and to make possible what appear to be changes in direction of the flow of life's process. We live in a world shaped by language and mythic stories *and* live subject to the forces of the events of our history and our future. Our lives are subject to the vicissitudes of the interactions between these two factors that tend to determine who we are.

This way of seeing (and, according to Ricoeur, at the same time not quite being able to see fully) the human situation of individuals and communities set in time means for pastoral practice that we must always take into account "facts," "forces," and "events," on the one hand, and "interpretations," "meanings," and "narrative accounts," on the other hand. I have used the quotation marks around each of these factors to indicate that our formulations concerning all of them are subject to the ambiguity of the impassable barrier to human understanding brought into focus by Ricoeur's time and narrative studies. Pastoral action in any human situation evoking our pastoral care must be action that responds to that situation. As Niebuhr has said in his explication of the theological ethics of the fitting response, the first question to be asked is the question, "What is happening here?" or "What is going on in this situation?" To approach making any kind of conjecture concerning the appropriate answer to those questions involves attention to both the historical, factual elements, and the narrative, meaning elements in the situation.[22]

It is likewise important for the pastor to keep in mind that, just as the life process of the individuals and communities under consideration are subject to the vicissitudes of the interplay of events and interpretations of events, so also are the processes that shape our responsive pastoral actions. We, too, participate in finitude. We, too, have had our consciousness shaped by the flow of events of our lives. We, too, have had our understanding of what is embraced by common sense molded by the communities and traditions in which we have lived. Our images concerning what constitutes sound judgment are embedded in the communal tradition that has most formatively shaped our vision of what the world is and should be. We do not have the advantage of making our determinations concerning what is happening or what is the most fitting response from some ahistorical, privileged position. Rather, our position is one better spoken of as that of the participant observer—the one who both participates in what is going on, and who seeks to observe what happens from a particular standpoint. Our intention is to observe and to participate primarily from the standpoint of the ideal community as informed by the tradition from which our pastoral identity has been granted us. We know, however, that other traditions, other events extraneous to the events of our ministry, and other storied ways of interpreting events will likewise have their influence on our conjecturing and our actions. So we, too, are limited, finite, hedged about by the vicissitudes of our lives.

THE NEIGHBORHOOD BOUNDARY PROBLEM REVISITED

Having distanced ourselves from the immediacy of the practical boundary problem that confronted a white suburban neighborhood by means of a theoretical detour into the aesthetic hermeneutics of Gadamer, the time and narrative studies of Ricoeur, and the theological ethics of responsibility of Niebuhr, we return now to the situation of praxis to see what fresh insights come into view. What can we now see that remained obscure before taking the detour?

The first and most obvious observation that these theories point to is the degree to which both participants appeal to common sense. Each appeals to what they seem to presume will be a concern held in common with the other. "We are concerned about the safety of our children." "This is a busy neighborhood and most of us park our own cars on the street. Furthermore . . ." Yet, there is also evidence of conflict concerning which action (the signing or the refusal to sign the petition) represents sound judgment in the situation. Is it stretching Gadamer's aesthetic hermeneutics too far to suggest that there may be two very different aesthetic visions and sets of ideals with regard to taste at work in the conversation? Does Niebuhr's emphasis upon the context within which human actions are to be considered suggest a significant difference in the perspectives of the two women?

One portrait of the ideal community clearly seems to be focused on privacy and safety from intrusion. The other perspective seems to emerge from an envisioned communal picture that is more open, even hospitable to the stranger who comes from outside. To the extent that this observation is accurate, we can say that there is an aesthetic of the fitting grounded in an understanding of the context to be considered at work beneath the surface of the actions of both parties, albeit sharply differing ones. To be sure, those differing aesthetic visions interact with differing histories of relational experience. The younger mother is quite apparently preoccupied with her immediate responsibility for small children, while the older woman's children are grown and gone from her immediate responsibility. Having lived through a longer history of child rearing, her perspective is perhaps more open to wider considerations.

Second, this little vignette from the life of an ordinary middle-class neighborhood illustrates dramatically the dangers inherent in the implicit trust placed by communities on judgments governed by common sense. Since 95 percent of the households in the community supported the parking restrictions, we can probably assume that the restriction represented the common sense (the sense held in common) of the vast majority of the community's residents. By their signing of the petition, that majority exercised a considerable degree of power not only over their neighbors who did not sign and must arrange for off-street parking for their vehicles, but also over a large group of persons they have never met who must now find other places to park their cars—or possibly even be deprived of after-school work necessitating the use of an automobile. In numerous similar ways, even in a democratic society, the right of a powerful majority to make the rule of its common sense the rule for all is exercised in ways that can be destructively oppressive to a minority whose common sense may be very different from that of the group in power. American society is becoming increasingly aware of the ways in which such exercise of the power of an unexamined common sense has functioned to keep alive practices such as racism and sexism in that society. What has been the case with those two now sharply visible flaws in the common sense of the society is without question likewise the case in countless less visible ways.

Third, the commonplace incident over the availability of street parking in this suburban community provides a down-to-earth, practical documentation of the reality that the task of transformation of a society at the point of its understanding of norms and boundaries involves the transformation of the contents of a society's common sense. It illustrates that it is the sense held in common by the people of a community that tends to rule the normative boundary decisions that are wittingly or unwittingly made in the ordinariness of everyday life together. If that is in fact generally the case, it therefore follows that transforming that community's life means transforming that common sense of who the people of the community are and who they envision themselves seeking to become. Does that not suggest that it is primarily in the arena of common sense that the church and its ministers must find their normative mission and ministry?

It is just at this point that the concepts of sound judgment and aesthetic taste—taken from Gadamer's aesthetic hermeneutics along with the concept of the fitting developed by means of a dialogue between Gadamer's aesthetics and Niebuhr's ethics of responsibility—become crucial as checks against the tyranny of a community's common sense. In Gadamer's aesthetics, sound judgment holds up before the common mind of the community the normative values of the deeper tradition that has shaped that community. In the manner of the prophets, sound judgment confronts the community with its own deepest wisdom, the wisdom of its originating narratives. Aesthetic taste confronts the community with a transcendent vision of the whole of that community's understanding of the world to which the parts of that world need to be made to conform. Niebuhr's ethics relocates the context within which the exercise of common sense takes place into the ultimate context of God's purpose and human participation in the fulfillment of divine purpose. That does not, to be sure, mean that the transcendent vision that shapes the norms of taste in a community should be seen as unchanging. As Gadamer himself says, "One does violence to the concept of taste if one does not include in it its variability. If it is anything, taste is a testimony to the changeableness of all human things and the relativity of all human values." Again we encounter the understanding of tradition as a living, human process that is constantly changing, while retaining deep continuities.[23]

Together, sound judgment and aesthetic taste provide a community with an ethic of the fitting. By means of that ethic, normative decisions may be made such that the actions and decisions of the community may not only fit together, but be fitting within the ongoing historical development of that community's grounding story of the ultimate context within which that community finds its meaning. From that perspective, the boundary decision being made by the suburban neighborhood may be seen as highly symbolic of that community's capacity and/or incapacity to change its common sense, reexamine the stories that give it its primary identity, and make a decision that is fitting in relation to a larger whole of which the community is a part.

AESTHETIC HERMENEUTICS AND PRACTICAL THEOLOGY

In my last book, I proposed the following definition of practical theology:

Practical theology . . . is the critical and constructive reflection on the life and work of Christians in all the varied contexts in which that life takes place with the intention of facilitating transformation of life in all its dimensions in accordance with the Christian gospel. Practical theology, seen from a narrative hermeneutical perspective, involves a process of the interpretive fusion of horizons of meaning embodied in the Christian narrative with other horizons that inform and shape perceptions in the various arenas of activity in which Christians participate.[24]

This definition makes possible a linkage with Gadamer's concepts of sound judgment and aesthetic taste, as well as the concept of the fitting as developed from the dialogue between Gadamer and Niebuhr. Placed alongside each other, these two structures of thought are suggestive of a major role or undertaking for the work of practical theology on the part of both church and ministry. It is the work of cultivation of the restorative power of sound judgment, aesthetic taste, and inquiry concerning the fitting—not only in the churches, but also in the larger community and culture as well. The transformation of communal life in all its dimensions is here seen as dependent upon the transformative recovery of wise judgment and a certain aesthetic taste in the Gadamerian sense at every level of our communal life. From the standpoint of Christian practical theology, such a recovery should be in accordance with the deepest and richest narrative themes of the Christian gospel in the style formulated by Niebuhr among those who claim that narrative tradition as their grounding story. Furthermore, in the pluralistic world in which Christians now find themselves, practical theology must take its place in the work of bringing about a fusion of horizons of the Christian source of judgment, taste, and understanding of the fitting with other horizons that shape differing views of judgment, taste, and the fitting in contemporary life.

What our analysis of the commonplace situation described in the story of the parking controversy suggests is that it is in just such ordinary everyday situations that the most important work of practical theology needs to be done. It is at this level of family, neighborhood, and community life that the common sense of the people operates to shape and perpetuate a way of life and relationship to the world. In our present situation of cultural fragmentation, this common sense of the people becomes threatened. The common sense of the people is less sure of itself. Its deep continuities become vulnerable and are called into question. Aberrations from the sense held in common appear—aberrations often not governed by either sound judgment or aesthetic good taste. In that fragmented situation, the boundaries and norms that govern the common life of the people become blurred for many. For others, frightened or angered by what appear to be the flaunting of common sense boundaries, the rule of common sense is powerfully reaffirmed in ways that are oppressive and closed against any and all efforts to bring about cultural transformation and change.

It is in just this increasingly fluid and fragmented situation as it is made evident in the the flow of events and conflicts occurring in individual, family, and community life that pastors and congregations are presented with the opportunity to engage in practical theological thinking and action. Within the framework developed in this chapter, that praxis will include a reexamination of many aspects of our common human life in

65

search of a recovered sense of the meaning content of sound judgment, aesthetic taste, and fitting response. The work of the pastor at all levels, including preaching, pastoral care, and congregational leadership, will in this situation be governed in large part by a disciplined effort to provide pastoral guidance to persons engaged in a new search for boundaries and norms. Reflection on ways in which that work of the pastor may be undertaken provides the agenda for the next chapter.

CHAPTER THREE

FROM IMAGINATION
TO METAPHOR:

Pastoral Care and the Transformation of Common Sense

W e began the work of the previous chapter with an expression of frustration: the frustration of a young pastor over what appeared to be the undisciplined way in which ordinary people make decisions about norms and boundaries. The pastor was having difficulty making connections between what had been observed in the day-to-day life of a parish community and the reasoned process of ethical reflection as it had been learned in a seminary classroom. Reflection on that dissonant observation pointed toward the notion that many, if not most, of the normative decisions of everyday life are made more in the mode of intuition—the exercise of imaginative common sense. Ordinary life tends to be governed more by the imagination than by reason, and to the extent that practical reasoning is involved, it seems more often to be governed by common sense wisdom rather than rational principles or logical rules of ethics.

Taking the baffled pastor's observation somewhat at face value, I turned our attention in chapter 2 toward testing that observation in relation to a commonplace situation of boundary conflict in a white, middle-class neighborhood. There we found some verification of what my young pastor friend observed: verification tempered, however, by a recognition that there was a degree of reasoned logic present in the conversation between two women over a street parking controversy. Upon reflection, it further appeared that the reasoning of the participants was linked to relational ties and imagistic memories. The case also revealed a community acting on a sense of the situation at hand held in common by a majority of its citizens.

PASTORAL GUIDANCE AND THE TRANSFORMATION
OF COMMON SENSE

By the end of chapter 2, a sense of direction for the work of pastoral care practice began to emerge from my effort to locate the popular cultural notion of common sense within the framework of Gadamer's aesthetic hermeneutics. That location links common sense to an aesthetic vision of the ideal community as that vision is shaped by a particular cultural tradition. It likewise links common sense to culturally derived notions of sound judgment, aesthetic taste, and a sense of the fitting, though that linkage is fraught with a certain prophetic tension between the sense common to the people, and the more fully normative sense expressed by those who exercise sound judgment and good taste. Thus, set within the background of Gadamer's aesthetics, an important purpose for pastoral practice began to take shape. Pastoral practice, most particularly pastoral practice in the situations of everyday life in which normative boundary issues are present, is rightly concerned with the transformation of common sense, the fostering of sound judgment, and the exercise of aesthetic taste. A primary focus for pastoral ministry began to clarify itself—a focus on the evocation of common practices that fit with the aesthetic vision contained in the primal story of the Christian community.

In my book, *Widening the Horizons*, I proposed an organizing image for the role of the pastor in the contemporary situation, namely, the image of the "interpretive guide." After pointing out that the image of pastoral guidance has a long history generally recognized as having its formative roots in the New Testament, I said:

> The guidance image seems to be worth preservation in an age in which persons are searching for sources of practical wisdom concerning ordinary problems of living that combine commitment to a structure of religious meaning and faith with knowledge of the complexities of modern life. It denotes a style of attending to the welfare of God's people in the modern pluralistic context that combines both leadership and nurturing care, both a certain pastoral wisdom in matters of importance for living and yet the recognition that the people of God are much of the time scattered in widely differing arenas of life about which the pastor has only limited knowledge. . . .
>
> I want to further qualify the image of guidance by associating it with the use of the term *interpreter* or *interpretive*. This qualification places a limit on the authority of the pastor in relation to command or direction and suggests that the most appropriate exercise of pastoral initiative in the modern context is at the point of interpretation of both the Christian narrative tradition and the contemporary living situations being confronted.[1]

Note that in describing what I meant by pastoral interpretive guidance I made reference to pastoral wisdom in the interpretation of both the Christian narrative tradition, and the contemporary situations encountered in ordinary life. It is this wisdom that the pastor attempts to offer in all the varied circumstances in which the pastor's guidance is sought by the people within her or his care. I want to link the concept of wise pastoral guidance first to Gadamer's aesthetic understanding of the function of wise judgment in relation to common sense. In Gadamer's aesthetic hermeneutics, wise judgment brings a certain normative perspective to its dialogue with common sense. It is a way of assessing the particular at hand by its relationship to the whole of things and the good of the whole community. It thus involves a certain wisdom in terms of what is fitting for the welfare of both individual and community.

To further borrow from Gadamer's pre-Kantian understanding of judgment:

It is clearly not only a matter of logical, but of aesthetic judgment. The individual case on which judgment works is never simply a case; it is not exhausted by being a particular example of a general law or concept. Rather, it is always an 'individual case,' and it is significant that we call it a special case, because the rule does not comprehend it. Every judgment about something that is intended to be understood in its concrete individuality, as the situations in which we have to act demand of us, is—strictly speaking—a judgment about a special case. That means simply that the evaluation of the case does not merely apply the measure of the universal principle according to which it is judged, but itself co-determines it, supplements and corrects it.[2]

Here we see how, for Gadamer, the exercise of judgment involves a kind of mutually critical dialogical relationship between the particular instance of human experience at hand and an aesthetic knowledge of the whole. It is not fully governed by principles of logic and reason, but entails the exercise of what Gadamer, following the pre-Kantian humanistic tradition—a tradition originating in Greek culture that had powerful influence on early Christian history—speaks of as taste.[3] To exercise taste is to have the imaginative capacity to discern what is fitting in relation to the whole of things as that whole has been seen by the best wisdom of a community's tradition.

I would remind you that in my own appropriation of Gadamer's notion of aesthetic judgment, I linked it in a dialogical fusion with H. Richard Niebuhr's concept of the fitting that is rooted primordially in Niebuhr's interpretation of the prophetic narratives of the Old Testament. With that added linkage to Niebuhr's biblically based understanding of the fitting, we may now say that the Christian pastor exercises wise and prophetically imaginative judgment in fulfilling the role of interpretive guidance. The pastor's exercise of that judgment is always to be responsible, that is, judgment in response to the needs of both the individual and the community by one who is also responsible for preserving the core wisdom of the Christian community's tradition. It attends both to the wisdom contained in the grounding narratives of the community *and* to the particularity of the community's situation in the present, fostering a mutually critical dialogue between them.

PASTORAL GUIDANCE AND THE PROPHETIC IMAGINATION

In his widely read book *The Prophetic Imagination*, the Old Testament scholar Walter Brueggemann provides a potently provocative model for the role of prophetic ministry in the contemporary world that is congruent in many ways with the Gadamerian/Niebuhrian model I have been seeking to develop. Early in his book, Brueggemann begins the explication of his model by asserting that the one who is to exercise prophetic imagination must sustain a continuing dialogue between contemporary life and the tradition that nurtures her or his ministry.

> It is the task of prophetic ministry to bring the claims of the tradition and the situation of enculturation into an effective interface. That is, the prophet is called to be a child of the tradition, one who has taken it seriously in the shaping of his or her own field of perception and system of language, who is so at home in that memory that the points of contact and incongruity with the situation of the church in culture can be discerned and articulated with proper urgency.[4]

In a footnote to this paragraph, Brueggemann acknowledges that "To be sure, the prophet lives in tension with the tradition. While the prophet is indeed shaped by the tradition, breaking free from the tradition to assert the new freedom of God is also characteristic of the prophet."[5] Again a certain congruence becomes evident among the three sources from which I am drawing—Gadamer, Niebuhr, and Brueggemann. It is that congruence that supports the image of the imaginative, prophetic, interpretive guide for the work of ministry in our time.

There is much more that could be taken over from Brueggemann's portrayal of the prophetic imagination, especially something akin to what I have underlined as the centrality of the transformation of common sense in relation to norms and boundaries as a purpose for the ministry of the church today. Brueggemann states the primary hypothesis of his book in a similar way: *"The task of prophetic ministry is to nurture, nourish, and evoke a consciousness and perception alternative to the consciousness and perception of the dominant culture around us."*[6] That task, Brueggemann goes on to say, is both a task of criticism of contemporary common sense culture and of energizing persons concerning the "promise of another time and situation toward which the community of faith may move . . . to live in fervent anticipation of the newness that God has promised and will surely give."[7]

Walter Brueggemann orients his conception of imaginative prophetic ministry not only to the obligations preserved in traditional Christian values and norms, but also to an appropriation of Christian eschatological expectation. The God of imaginative prophetic ministry is an active God who is ever in process of bringing about new and transforming reality. God is God not only of the past, but also of the present and the future, as well. Prophetic ministry must therefore be attuned to the transformations of life that God is bringing about. Its purpose is oriented to the creation of that new reality, not simply to the preservation of the old. Prophetic ministry keeps before it a vision of the possible toward which God is actively calling God's people.

Much more work remains to be done before a clearly defined methodology for the exercise of imaginative prophetic pastoral guidance begins to take shape. As a matter of fact, since the model I am attempting to bring before my readers is one dependent on the functioning of intuitive imagination, it will in all probability never reduce itself to anything like a step-by-step methodology that can be simply applied to all situations. In that sense, what I am seeking to bring to disclosure will reveal itself to be more of an art form than a methodology. In fundamental ways, it is an aesthetic practice, not a technique to be followed in the solution of practical problems. In more traditional theological language, imaginative prophetic pastoral guidance is a calling, a pilgrimage of discernment, that is dependent upon and to be exercised as a gift of God. It is dependent upon the imaginative opening of a way of response to the contemporary situation of God's people in reaction to the leading of the Spirit. The imaginative prophetic pastor will seek to both embody and respond to the wisdom of God as that wisdom has been made available to us in the stories of our tradition and as that wisdom reveals itself to us in the events and issues of our present life.

71

AN EXAMPLE OF UNANTICIPATED PROPHETIC
PASTORAL GUIDANCE

Before proceeding further with the development of the model of imaginative prophetic pastoral guidance, it may be useful to have before us an example of what I have in mind. What would this artistic practical theologian look like? In a meditation for World Communion Sunday, 1988, Howard Wall, a minister, relates the following story:

Two women were walking down the aisle to receive the symbols of the body and blood of Jesus Christ. These women represented a conflict that in the previous months had torn apart the church, the community and me. This conflict was a small version of a broader one that had troubled our nation for a decade and today still plagues many parts of the world.

This particular crisis began one Saturday afternoon. I was dressing for a wedding when the telephone rang. The caller, named Mary, said she was a Presbyterian who had recently moved into our area from New Jersey. She had attended a Baptist church near where she now lived, but really had not felt at home there. Could she attend our church?

"Of course," I replied. "Everyone is always welcome at our church."

Those words came out automatically. Churches in every community I had lived in said the same thing. "Everyone is always welcome" was understood by people in each community to mean "everyone like us." The fact that this woman felt she had to ask indicated that either she did not understand unspoken rules or she intended to test them.

As I was going out the door the telephone rang again. This time it was a young woman who was a member of my church. She spoke with some agitation. "The woman you just talked to—she called from my house. Did you know that she is black?"

"No, but I wondered," I replied.

"It isn't my fault," she continued. "She came over to use my phone. Then she saw the offering envelopes on the coffee table. I told her we had a friendly church and that you were such a good minister. And she said that she was a Presbyterian, and . . ."

"Don't worry; you did what was right," I assured her.[8]

I interrupt Pastor Wall's story at this point to suggest that we as readers of it reflect as we go along on its implications for imaginative prophetic ministry. Following Niebuhr's suggestion that the first question to ask about any human situation should concern what is happening, I want carefully, yet imaginatively and intuitively, to examine the movement of this story to see what it has to tell us about the transformation of common sense by prophetic imagination. What is going on in this story?

In many respects, this story is not an unusual one in the life of churches all across the American South over the last twenty-five years. More than a few congregations have been confronted with the necessity of coming to terms with the contradiction between their commitment to welcome strangers into their midst and their overt or covert racism. As Pastor Wall suggests early on in his story, the inclusive norms of the Gospel in this regard have often been so skewed by the common sense norms of the community that the "Everyone Welcome" slogan has come to be encoded to mean "Everyone Like Us Welcome." But almost inevitably, often, as in this case, incidents unexpectedly have occurred that forcibly presented the issue. The result has not always been salutary. Congregations caught in the midst of communities in economic and racial transition have more often than not dwindled in their impact on the life of those communities because of white flight and/or refusal to open their doors to the strangers at their gates. Sometimes whole congregations have folded their tents and sought a new location where "our people come from," which when decoded means, "where there are more people like ourselves and fewer strangers."

Pastor Wall continues:

The wedding with which I assisted was held in a large Baptist church about five miles from the church I served. Perhaps I was just in a bad mood, but I did not enjoy that celebration. The wedding cake symbolized my perception of the whole affair. It was huge, expensive and garishly decorated, with tasteless layers and sickeningly sweet icing.

Later that evening I learned that this was the church Mary had attended. She had been invited first to witness the baptism of a neighbor's daughter. After she attended the next two Sundays, the minister was warned in an anonymous telephone call that the church and/or parsonage would be burned down "if that nigger keeps coming to church." (Within a year, however, the congregation voted that people of all races would be welcome at their worship services.)

But what would happen at the small church I served? It was located in what had been until after World War II an isolated fishing village. Most of the residents were descendants of English peasants and sailors who had settled on the coast of the New World in the late colonial period. They were warm and friendly to people once they got to know them, but they would not choose to be in the forefront of social change.

The only black woman who had ever lived within three miles of the church was married to a white soldier. People who upheld community

73

tradition seldom spoke to her, and when they did it was with the sort of benevolent bewilderment that others might display toward the village idiot or the town drunk.

We again interrupt Pastor Wall's story to begin a series of reflections upon it, treating the story as a paradigmatic one that may disclose a series of generalizations about the occurrence of opportunities for imaginative prophetic ministry in ordinary situations.

1. The first thing we notice is that the occasion for the exercise of prophetic ministry arises unexpectedly in the normal flow of everyday events.

As Pastor Wall relates it, the beginning of this incident that drew him and his congregation into the situation of having to reconsider their common-sense norms came with an unexpected telephone call that interrupted his dressing for a wedding. Furthermore, the description of the circumstances surrounding the making of that telephone call by Mary, the stranger in the community, make it appear almost (though not quite) as a random event initiated by Mary on an impulse. She just happened to come to a neighbor's house to use the phone and happened to notice her neighbor's offering envelopes on the coffee table. On impulse, Mary, who had been disappointed in her efforts to find a church in a new community, decided to call the pastor of her neighbor's church to see if she would be welcome there. All of that series of happenings seems at first glance almost casual, certainly ordinary. Yet not quite, because they quickly begin to be given a force and purpose originating in Mary's desire for a church in which she could feel at home. A hint of human loneliness, alienation, and pain gently enters the atmosphere of the story. "Could I attend your church?" We see both Mary's desire and her anticipation of rejection.

Quickly, the commonplace event of the telephone call begins to gather around it a quiet but distinct drive toward a more than commonplace significance. The telephone call from Mary is followed by a call from the church member-neighbor. "It isn't my fault. . . . I told her we had a friendly church and that you were such a good minister." The neighbor thus reveals her ambivalence. Is she at fault for recommending her church and pastor to a black woman? The common-sense coding of friendly has been violated, albeit somewhat inadvertently. One senses that she is caught in a double violation: the over-stepping of a common-sense norm and a faint but definite recognition that there is a deeper, more authentic norm that the common-sense encoding may violate.

2. *The moment for prophetic ministry response arises at the time of the recognition that human suffering and conflict have appeared.*

In Pastor Wall's story, he did not himself initiate the action of the story that began the transformation of his church community's common sense. Rather, the transformative action began with a cry of human pain and loneliness on the part of Mary and a conflicted reaction to that cry on the part of Mary's neighbor. Is this not most often the case? Is not the first initiative toward prophetic, transforming action most often an action of the aggrieved, those who are in one way or another the ones whom the common-sense norm has violated? Was this not so with the children of Israel? As Walter Brueggemann puts it in his reflections on the Exodus texts: "The grieving of Israel, perhaps self-pity and surely complaint but never resignation, is the beginning of criticism."[9]

For those of us who are pastors, this fundamental characteristic of situations in which the need for transformation of common sense is present suggests what might well be considered a rule or at least a rule-of-thumb. It places before us the necessity that we ever be on the alert to hear the cry of suffering and violation, no matter how faintly it is expressed or how conflicted the expression of that cry may be. Imaginative prophetic ministry is virtually always responsive ministry. It awaits alertly the cry of pain that may come at the most unexpected time and in the most unexpected manner. It hears that cry and responds. "Of course. Everyone is always welcome at our church."

I would dare to venture that many pastors who have either been overcome in their efforts to be faithful to the Gospel by their own unconscious observance of the rule of common sense norms in the communities in which they minister, or who have failed in their efforts to confront injustice, or other blatant violation of fundamental values, have done so in large part because of their failure to hear and respond to the cries of those who are suffering. Prophetic ministry requires interaction between those who are in pain and those who see the need for change. And very often, the change that is needed is change in the common sense of the people.

Later in the story, Pastor Wall speaks of his surprise at finding that one of the lay people who makes the first move to accept Mary, the black stranger, into the congregation is Jan, a widow who had herself known suffering in the course of rearing a large family alone. As is often the case, the past suffering of one resonates with the suffering of another in ways that break through the barriers of common-sense practices in the community. It is interesting, though a bit puzzling, that Pastor Wall, in telling of Jan's participation in the prophetic crisis, speaks of her history of suffering as an excuse for her liberal attitude. Why, we wonder, does he tell the story in that so patently insensitive manner? Although we cannot with certainty answer that question, we can tentatively speculate that we may see revealed a small, but significant indication of Pastor Wall's frustration that there are not more of his people willing to share the prophetic burden of the crisis time. If that is the case, we are reminded that bearing the responsibility of prophetic leadership involves a quality of suffering fraught with ambivalence, uncertainty, and the wish for support. The prophetic pastor, too, can become involved in complaint.

3. Once heard, the cry of pain begins to transform the consciousness of the imaginative prophetic pastor.

An important episode in Pastor Wall's story is the episode of the wedding in which he assisted immediately following the telephone calls. It was in most respects an ordinary wedding—a bit more ostentatious than some, to be sure, but not unusual for this community. But for Pastor Wall, that wedding took on a new and peculiar appearance. It was as if he was seeing what was happening through new lenses. He was somehow repelled by it. From the story we can conjecture that his changed consciousness was in ways not easy to define connected with the telephone calls he had just received.

Having noted the shift in Pastor Wall's perception of the expensive ostentation of the wedding *in which he was a participant*, intuitive reflection opens before us the possibility that Pastor Wall began at the wedding to experience *himself as the stranger* in his own cultural context. In the flow of events in which he had participated—the telephone calls, the wedding and reception following it—he had been given a fresh awareness of the extent to which the commonly accepted culture of ordinary life in his community was out of harmony with the vision of what human life might and should be to which he was committed. Seen from the perspective provided by the Gadamerian/Niebuhrian frame of reference with which we have been working, Pastor Wall's aesthetic interpretation of the wedding feast judged it to be unfit. Ordinarily, he might well have participated in that celebration without paying it much attention. It was not that unusual. But his perceptions had been sharpened. He had been reminded of the deep flaws in the portrait of the good life that his culture's shared vision of it painted. The painful gap between common-sense culture and his normative vision of the good and righteous community had been laid bare, and laid bare by the confluence of some very ordinary occurrences in a busy pastor's life.

Even though we are dealing with mundane events such as a woman's search for a friendly church and an ostentatious wedding, it is well to remind ourselves of a certain correspondence between Pastor Wall's situation and that of the Old Testament prophets. They, too, were by and large very ordinary persons doing very ordinary things who began to see the commonly accepted practices of their people through the lenses of an alternative consciousness. They, too, took on the consciousness of the stranger, no longer at home with the commonly accepted practices of their people, most particularly their community's leaders. Yet they remained a part of the Israelite community and spoke their prophetic message as persons dedicated to the larger vision to which that community was called. They spoke their prophetic messages to the community from within that community, yet they spoke as from the distance of an outside perspective that could see it as a flawed whole. Their message was a message to call Israel back to a vision that was fitting, given their origins.

At this point in the story, Pastor Wall makes an important decision.

On Saturday evening I spoke to all the elders to explain the situation to them. None of them shouted Hallelujah! One expressed fear that this woman was part of a conspiracy, and that if she came one Sunday, the next Sunday there would be a dozen blacks at services not to worship but to make trouble. Another worried that Mary's participation might cause a drop in contributions. . . . However one of the newly elected women elders volunteered to bring Mary to church.

Two minutes before the prelude on Sunday morning Mary slipped in quietly and sat on a back pew. As we began the service, the congregation was tense and quiet. It was as if we were on a small boat, drifting over a dangerous shoal. Everyone was afraid to make a sudden move or speak above a whisper for fear that even such slight disturbances could cause the craft to lurch against the sharp rocks that lay hidden just below the waves.

We made it through that Sunday, and through a dozen succeeding Sundays without an obvious incident. A few people began to speak politely to Mary; others obviously avoided her. Some hoped that she would quietly disappear.

However, this was not to be. Mary began attending the church membership class I taught, and on the Sunday before Christmas she joined our church.

I was, in general, very proud of how the congregation accepted this. One of the people who pleasantly surprised me was Jan. Her only excuse for being a "liberal" in this matter was that the pain and suffering she had endured as an aging widow who had reared a large family alone had purged her heart of the pride that prevents people from loving and understanding others.

One evening I visited Sam and Margie. I often thought of Sam as the Big Fisherman. He seldom spoke in church meetings, but when he did nobody argued with him. He had scuttled more than one proposed course of action by stating, "It's just not right!"

When we moved into the living room for our conversation, I knew it would be a serious one. Sam told me who in the church was most upset, and the comments that some were making about going to another church or canceling pledges of financial support. Then he said, "This has been my church for 40 years, and nobody is going to keep me away. But with Margie it is different."

Margie joined in. "I just can't go back. I wasn't brought up that way. It doesn't seem like the same church any more. I can't go back."

She wasn't angry, she was afraid. It was as if her husband was trying to walk on water, and though he might not drown, she knew what would happen if she tried.

Margie had been taking care of the communion service. Before I left she brought me a box containing the communion utensils and suggested that someone else take over this responsibility.

For the following seven or eight months, Sam came to church alone. Then one Sunday Margie came and sat in her usual seat beside Sam on the next-to-the-last row. I never asked what caused her to change her mind, but was pleased to see her in her seat every Sunday up through World Communion Sunday.

I would suggest that we again back away from our immediate involvement in Pastor Wall's narrative to continue the formulation of general principles of imaginative prophetic ministry. This last episode in the story seems to suggest the following:

4. Beginning very early in the movement of events toward the prophetic moment, the imaginative prophetic pastor is called upon to exercise sound judgment.

A crucial moment of prophetic pastoral practice began for Pastor Wall when his conflict-ridden parishioner called him to report that she had referred Mary, the black woman, to her church and to Pastor Wall. His response was immediate: "Don't worry. You did what was right." Clearly this response rings true as representing judgment backed by wisdom. Just as clearly, it has the ring of an intuitive judgment. It does not come after weighing all the alternatives or after checking the neighbor's behavior by any code of rules. Rather, it came as an intuitive, wise reassurance from one who spoke with the authority of moral leadership.

Crucial as that exercise of sound judgment was, it was not to be the last, or even perhaps the most important one. At a number of critical points in the sequence of events that followed, Pastor Wall acted in ways that evidence a similar degree of sound judgment.

The second wise decision was to speak with the elders of the congregation about what was happening prior to the first Sunday Mary was likely to appear in the congregation for worship. Pastor Wall wisely elected to share the responsibility for the prophetic moment with the recognized lay leaders of the community rather than go it alone, and he chose to provide a forum within which the community leaders could begin to struggle with their responsibility for the community, its vision of itself, and its future response to what was occurring.

Although Pastor Wall does not speak in his description of the meeting with the elders of the participation of God in what was happening, from reading the entire story it is apparent that he was developing a growing awareness that God was actively involved. "God, why are you doing this to (us)?" Here Pastor Wall reveals his identification with the people of the congregation. In the confluence of events, God was at work in their midst, and at work in ways that in certain respects set God against them and they against God. Pastor Wall's wisdom stands somewhere between God on the one side, and Pastor Wall and his congregation, on the other. Pastor Wall wisely chose not to attempt to speak for God, but rather to assume the role of the interpretive guide shepherding his people through a time and situation of prophetic importance.

One consequential result of Pastor Wall's decision to share the responsibility for the prophetic moment with his lay leaders was that, in the midst of all of the nay-saying of cautious adherents to the dominant common sense of the community with regard to racial matters, one newly elected female elder volunteered to share publicly the prophetic responsibility with Pastor Wall. She would bring Mary to church. What is included in the story tells us only a little about her motivation, but we can with some confidence conjecture that she would not have stepped forward to join her pastor in taking prophetic responsibility had he chosen to approach the elders in a more confrontational, less participative fashion. With her, Pastor Wall had succeeded in inviting a shared praxis of prophetic imagination!

5. The imaginative prophetic pastor, rather than precipitously forcing the confrontation of the issue(s) at stake in the prophetic episode, assumes a stance that is pastoral, allowing the issue(s) to emerge as it (they) will in the community's life together.

It is no doubt significant that in the thickening of the plot of Pastor Wall's congregation's confrontation with their racism there are no reports of sharp, potentially divisive confrontations between Pastor Wall and any of his congregants. We can surmise that everyone knew where he stood on the issue. He had received Mary into the congregation. He had given his pastoral blessing to the invitation issued by Mary's neighbor. He reports at the beginning of the story that the conflict "had torn apart the church, the community, *and me*" (emphasis mine). These were indeed tense and conflicted times in the life of this community of Christians! But rather than standing over against the community with an air of accusation and self-righteous aloofness, Pastor Wall acknowledges that he too was torn apart. Again we see him, like the prophets of Israel, as deeply and faithfully involved in and committed to the community in which he ministers.[10]

Pastor Wall does report a brief but very revealing vignette of his pastoral care ministry with one couple in the congregation, Sam and Margie. Sam is presented as a strong and perhaps somewhat unpredictable character who was known to be one who seldom speaks in church meetings, but to speak with great force of conviction when he decided to do so. "He had scuttled more than one proposed course of action by stating, 'it's just not right!'" From that reported observation alone we sense that Sam was very likely seen as one of the recognized figures of wise judgment in the community. One also senses that his judgments issued from some deeply felt vision of what was right and fitting, rather than from carefully exercised logical thought.

The Sam and Margie household is unfortunately divided on the issues of this time in the church's life. When the chips are down, Margie is presented as a strong and stubborn adherent to the codes and protocols of the common sense culture of her community. "I wasn't brought up that way. I can't go back." She even surrenders to her pastor the cherished communion utensils that had been in her care for a long time. A choice had been made: a choice to conform to common sense. With Sam it was different. One senses that he, too, is not fully comfortable with what seems a violation of accustomed practices in regard to race. But, stubbornly wise in his own way, he refuses to be forced to choose between his church and common-sense conformity. "This has been my church for 40 years, and nobody is going to keep me away." Sam, however, is sympathetic to Margie's loyalties. He is willing to accept her decision to withdraw. He will attend church alone.

It is significant that Pastor Wall does not argue the issues with either Sam or Margie. One senses that he listened and waited. Patiently, he allowed this little sub-plot of the story of his community to develop as it would. His response to Sam and Margie is caring, accepting, and non-judgmental. Given his understanding that God was actively involved in what was going on, we can conjecture that he was content to walk beside Sam and Margie while God's work with them moved at its own pace. Meanwhile, he remained pastorally faithful.

In a book written during the late 1960s at the height of the racial crisis in the American South, Wayne Oates, himself a product of mid-twentieth-century southern culture, wrote with deep conviction and great wisdom of the prophetic power of faithful pastoral care. Persons who receive faithful, consistently non-judgmental and deeply personal caring ministry in times of stress develop, says Oates, a profound trust in the pastor that provides a certain interpersonal leverage that is powerfully influential, even in areas of concern quite unrelated to the stress for which care was originally given. Used wisely, that leverage can open the way to the initiating of significant attitudinal and convictional change. From Pastor Wall's brief description of his relationship with Sam and Margie, we can surmise that this is precisely what was happening in their situation. Pastor Wall did not have to argue the merits of either Sam's or Margie's decision. His pastoral caring spoke for itself, and thereby influenced the ultimate direction of the transformations taking place in Margie's attitudes. His care no doubt likewise was significant in assisting Sam, the often stubborn and outspoken one, to exercise restraint and patient forbearance with Margie's conflict of conscience.[11]

Pastor Wall's story moves toward its dramatic conclusion:

> Communion had come to have a growing significance for me and the church. We had studied it in Sunday school and church membership classes. For a year we had been using the liturgy in the worshipbook. Families in the church took turns baking a large loaf to be shared in the service. A widow had donated a chalice, pitcher and plates for the bread in memory of her husband. We set up tables before the front pew and invited worshipers to sit at table to receive the elements.
>
> On World Communion Sunday, everything seemed to be ready when I checked just before the prelude. The larger-than-usual congregation included both Mary and Margie.
>
> The service seemed to move quickly to communion. I gave the invitation to the Lord's Table: "Friends, this is the joyful feast of the people of God. Many will come from east and west, from north and south, and sit at the table in the kingdom of God."

It soon became apparent that too many were coming. We were running out of cups, and at least a dozen people in the back rows had not been served. I whispered quietly to the person in charge of serving, "We need more cups!"

"We don't have any more!" she replied in a loud whisper.

What were we to do? A sudden inspiration came to me, and I shared it with the congregation immediately. "We have run out of cups. It is not a Presbyterian tradition, but I invite all those who have not been served, and are willing, to partake of a common cup, the chalice." (I had poured wine into the chalice as a symbolic gesture.)

A dozen people started coming forward. I could hardly believe it when I realized that Mary would be sitting on the end of the front pew beside Margie when I served the cup.

In my heart I thought, "God, why are you doing this to me? I had planned such a beautiful day to honor your name, and you conspired to use it all to destroy me. Open up the floor and let me fall straight into the flames of hell, and get it over with now!"

When I gave the chalice to Mary, she cradled it gently, drank and passed the chalice to Margie. Margie drank and passed the cup to her husband. He drank, as did all the others at the table. Then all returned quietly to their pews for the closing hymn and benediction.

As the choir sang "Amen" I went to the door of the sanctuary, and as the congregation began to file out I prayed, "Lord, let now your servant depart in peace; for my eyes have seen your salvation."[12]

In this dramatic ending, Pastor Wall's story reveals a turn in a direction that responds to Pastor Wall's prophetic ministry and the events that made his ministry possible. Although we may surmise that the issue of inclusivity is and will remain a lively one in this community, a new reality may be in the process of coming to be. An important step has been taken. The common sense of the people has begun to change. The "stranger at the gates" has been accepted into the "feast of the people of God."

From the story of the communion service it is possible to glean what appears to be a culminative principle of imaginative prophetic ministry.

6. The imaginative prophetic pastor both searches for and creates opportunities for metaphorical interaction between the story of the situation at hand and the primal mythic narratives of the Christian tradition. In doing so, the prophetic pastor likewise is alert to the gratuitous, unexpected appearance of metaphorical and parabolic situations that can, if artistically utilized, bring the issues at stake in the prophetic moment into metaphorical

82

relationship with the deepest images and themes of the grounding stories of the community.

We come to the climactic event in the story of Pastor Wall's congregation's prophetic confrontation with a choice between the realization of a transformed sense of their life together and adherence to the boundaries of their common sense culture. Like a highly condensed drama of mythic proportions, the story of the World Communion service unfolds. All of the principal characters in the story are present: Sam and Margie, undoubtedly Jan, Mary, and the anonymous neighbor who first invited the stranger into their midst, and, as the symbolic priestly head of the community, Pastor Wall. Most significant for the prophetic meaning of this celebration of the "feast of the people of God" was Mary's presence. Mary, the one with whom, by one of the strictest rules of Old South common-sense culture, the people of the congregation were forbidden to sit at the table.

These were the principal characters in the immediate drama of the communion service. But in this drama they were joined powerfully and symbolically by the Presence of Another. This was the Lord's table; these elements were symbolically "Christ's body broken for you" and "Christ's blood shed for you." In its metaphorical, symbolic meaning, the communion celebration transported the reality of the congregation's conflicted situation into another context, the context of the central story of the Christian community. In that context, the authority to command obedience of common-sense norms was revealed as not only a false authority, but also as one to be overcome.

It is crucially important to note that the actions of the critical moment of choice in the metaphorical drama of the communion service were quite unplanned. The situation was not created by Pastor Wall's contrivance. As the story unfolded, they simply ran out of cups at the very time when Mary and Margie, seemingly by chance, were to be at the table together. What was Pastor Wall to do? What he describes in his story of the event as a sudden inspiration came to Pastor Wall. He would invite the remaining unserved congregants to share the common symbolic cup. Only then did he realize the double significance of what was about to occur. Mary and Margie would be asked to serve each other from that cup, now powerfully symbolic of their common humanity. The merged metaphorical meaning of what they were to do with and for each other was unmistakable—and publicly so.

It is equally important to note that, right until the end, until Mary, Margie, Sam the Big Fisherman, and all the others had quietly shared in the feast and returned to their pews, Pastor Wall resisted and feared the

83

worst consequences of what was taking place. He had become merely the half-willing, half-unwilling participant, and not the architect of the drama that was unfolding in their midst. The double-leveled story, with its dramatic, metaphorical enactment of both the present and the traditional meanings of the event, had taken over. The prophetic moment had brought itself to its climax. All Pastor Wall had to do was allow it to happen. The responsibility for it was now not entirely his. "Lord, let now your servant depart in peace; for my eyes have seen your salvation."

Thus, the shared story ends. But in reality, we may be sure, the story continued and is continuing. Much pastoral and prophetic work remained to be done in the weeks and months that followed the climactic World Communion service. The context within which the continuing story is to take place is, however, significantly altered. It now moves into the future within the memory of the transformation of common sense that took place in the prophetic moment when the meaning of Mary's presence and the congregation's acceptance of her presence—most particularly her acceptance by Margie, the one who had acted out the congregation's loyalty to common-sense norms—was dramatically enacted. The vision of the ideal community contained in the congregation's primal narratives has been experienced metaphorically in the imagination of the people. Imaginatively and metaphorically, the power of the common-sense norms has been broken. What remains yet to unfold is how and to what extent Pastor Wall and his congregation can keep the memory alive, and live their life together in its transformed context of meaning.

METAPHORICAL THEMATA AND THE LINKING OF PRIMARY AND PRESENT-DAY STORIES

In Pastor Wall's story of the painful but dramatic transformation of the common-sense boundaries of his congregation's sense of its community, the link that the World Communion service provided between the primary story of the Lord's Supper and the present-day story of acceptance or rejection of the stranger in their midst is central. That link provided the impetus to change. They were simultaneously able to be a new community and a community in deep continuity with a primal story of their origins. It becomes important, therefore, that we examine more closely the role that metaphorical themes play in the transformation of an individual's or a community's common sense of itself.

In an interdisciplinary study of how innovations in both scientific and religious ways of thinking take place entitled *Metaphoric Process: The Creation of Scientific and Religious Understanding*, Mary Gerhart, a professor of religious studies, and Allen M. Russell, a professor of physics, speak of the presence in both science and religion of what they call "themata."

> In both science and religion, themata constitute the major cognitive structures of epistemological significance. In our conception of science and religion as fields of meanings, we shall expect to find that a thema, such as vitalism in science or theism in religion, will be variously expressed within a particular tradition of science or religion. Within either religion or science understood cross-culturally, themata that are affirmed and rejected appear, disappear, and reappear in a variety of motifs. Invariably, however, the cognitive structures of major meanings and issues—of themata—remain.[13]

A major characteristic of metaphorical themata, according to Gerhart and Russell, is that they "force us to examine the underlying continuities between seemingly disparate concepts. . . . 'Themata are not proved or disproved. Rather they rise and fall and rise again with the tides of contemporary usefulness.'"[14] Themata, therefore, may be seen as providing a sense of deep continuity with primary images and themes of a grounding narrative of a cultural community, while yet allowing the contemporary experience to initiate a reconsideration of the theme. The present experience clustered around the theme is both like and not like the human experience clustered around the originating narrative theme.[15] Thus, both the movement of change *and* the deep continuity of a cultural set of meanings is carried forward in life within a tradition through time.

If we carefully examine the two stories that are brought into juxtaposition through the enactment of the World Communion service in Pastor Wall's church, several themata are present. Most primary perhaps is the theme of the mystery of God's presence among God's people. In both stories, it is a presence celebrated but mysteriously both hidden and revealed: a commanding, yet mysterious reality both revered and not fully understood. In the originating story, the presence of God is made concrete and immediate by the presence of Jesus as the Son of God. In the immediate story, God is present in the symbols of the bread and wine, the body and blood of Christ.

There are other themata that can be readily identified in both stories as well, among them the theme of suffering and rejection, of acceptance and refusal of acceptance, of eating and drinking at the table set for the community, and, finally, the painful theme hovering in the background—that of suffering. Following Gerhart and Russell, we may say that these themata provided the vehicle by which the grounding story of this church and its community could be connected with the story of its immediate situation. Through the fusion of horizons of those two stories, the meaning context of the situational story could undergo transforming change.[16]

It is around three such metaphoric themata that are prominent in the narratives of the biblical, and later Christian theological, tradition that I want to build the work of the final three chapters of this book. I believe that they are also central metaphoric themes implicit, though often hidden, in many of the contemporary problematic situations being confronted by Christians in the world in which fundamental issues concerning norms, boundaries, and visions of the good life are at stake. They are the themata of *presence*, of *community*, and of *vocation*.

A CAUTIONARY ADDENDUM

Before turning to the work of those chapters, however, it seems important that I add a brief addendum to the work we have done in this chapter with the case of Pastor Wall's church and its encounter with Mary, the black stranger. In certain respects this case study, as it was presented, was an ideal prototype or model of an ideal possibility, rather than a typical or usual one. Its story is an ideal story of how prophetic ministry can take place, and the prophetic moment in a community's life can realize fulfilling transformation. As such, it facilitated identification of several of the ideal elements to be sought and capitalized on in all such situations calling for prophetic ministry. Problematic as it was, however, it did—in ways that could not have been planned or perhaps even imagined by Pastor Wall or his people—take crucial turns that moved it toward its apparently happy and normatively fitting conclusion.

The addendum is simply that it is not always thus! As we shall see as other specific situations appear in later pages of this book, more often than not the movement of the stories of immediate, critical human situations is more visibly ambiguous than was the movement of Pastor Wall's story. Not only are human situations encountered in ministry most often fundamentally ambiguous, fraught with both hopeful, positive elements and potentially destructive, despairing, negative trends, but also the thematic connections between the immediate and the primal stories are often not nearly so clear as they were in Pastor Wall's story. Making those connections will often be so difficult and tenuously complex as to tax the creative, prophetic imagination of any pastor. The normative issues in the situation at hand are often deeply buried under the flotsam and jetsam of cluttered individual, familial, and communal lives. Furthermore, the unplanned events that occur in the course of living out the story of the encounter with the prophetic moment are as often as not complicating, even obstructing and fragmenting events, rather than the fortuitous ones that occurred in Pastor Wall's story. The caution I wish to leave is: Do not expect all situations to be ideal or to have as unambiguously good and right endings as the one we have worked with in this chapter. And remember that, even in this situation, Pastor Wall until the end, anticipated not transformation, but disaster!

PART TWO

CHAPTER FOUR

NORMATIVE METAPHORS FOR PASTORAL WORK:

Presence

Readers who have followed the argument of this book through to this point will have become aware that I am attempting to propose fresh and imaginative ways in which pastoral care can contribute to an age-old ministerial task, the task of assisting persons and congregations to be and become the people of God in the world. That intention is directed particularly toward those pastors and congregations who are seeking genuine engagement with the cultural challenges and confusions that are so subtly but powerfully omnipresent in the ordinary flow of everyday life in North America. Many of those challenges and confusions have to do with competitive claims and eroding conceptualizations of what is right, true, and normative for human life. Human life needs boundaries and rules, norms and consensual values. It needs a more or less commonly held vision of what is good and true and beautiful, a life to be sought after and shared. Without these commonly held understandings, life becomes chaotic and unsafe. But, however we may wish it were not the case, many of what seem in our short human memory to be traditional norms and values don't seem to be working very well in the relativized and radically pluralistic context of contemporary life. A new or renewed search for norms seems urgently necessary.

I am writing particularly, I suppose, for pastors and parishioners who have come to believe that the old moralisms and moralistic ways of reasoning that governed much of common Christian religious and communal life in North America for decades in the earlier years of our century aren't working very well either, though there are still many persons in Christian congregations across North America who think of the Christian life largely in terms of some narrowly conceived set of moralistic rules and images of righteous piety. Some of us at times wish

91

that these moralisms were still in control of our life together, but all about us we see evidence that this is not the case.

I am proposing a fresh tack on the effort of the churches to reform and transform our culture's hold on a life lived within normative boundaries that has to do with carefully examining the manner in which ordinary life tends to be governed by common sense. I have argued that common sense is always rooted in some deeply formative narrative tradition that shapes a communal/cultural aesthetic vision of what the desirable, good, and appropriate life should be. It is a vision nurtured and kept alive in often inchoate form more by the imagination than by reason and logical argumentation. So we have looked together in the earlier chapters at how by the use of imagination and metaphor the common sense of the people can be given prophetic ministry.

AN AESTHETICS WITH THREE THEMATA

In making the turn away from moralisms and moralistic preoccupations toward more imagistic, aesthetic, and imaginative ways of thinking about the shape of the Christian life, I have found my attention being drawn again and again toward three clusters of images that gather around them many of the normative issues and questions of ordinary life in our time. At the end of the last chapter, I listed them as images of presence, of community, and of vocation. I am drawn to these three themata in part because in our present cultural situation they seem to encapsulate many of the deep longings and frustrated wishes of many people who are caught in the fragmentation and confusion of contemporary American culture.

In the age of the self in which the pursuit of narcissism seems to have become increasingly burdensome rather than satisfying, many people—particularly among the young—express a profound longing for a richer, more authentically human vision of what it means to be a person fully present in the world. Closely related to that deep longing may be seen a renewed desire for relationships in community. All about one is evidence of the search for ways of being together that transcend the instrumental ways of being crammed together in assembly lines, commuter trains, grid-locked expressways, condo developments, and anonymous apartments. Perhaps most of all, we long for ways of being in community that transcend the corporate business and bureaucratic organizations that structure so much of present-day life. What does it mean to live in communities together and in a community of nations of differing cultures? Hidden in both those clusters of human desire lies the question of vocation. Is it possible for ordinary persons in such a crammed together, cluttered and contentious, "get what you can" time to experience a renewed sense of vocation that can transcend the survivalist mentality that hovers over American culture?[1]

These three themes that I have selected as characteristic of the confused present-day search for a renewed aesthetic vision of what human life should be have precursors in the long history of human life. They are themes that have deep and rich antecedents in the Bible. They are themata that occur with varying emphasis and differentiated meaning throughout the history of the Christian community and its tradition. In times other than ours, they appeared in ways shaped by the historical circumstances. So in our own time they appear with the coloration provided by the realities of society and culture of the late twentieth century: The circumstances that shape the conditions with which we must make our engagement with life.

My suggestion is that careful and imaginative retrieval of the images and themes related to presence, community, and vocation found in the originating texts of our tradition can, when brought into dialogical relationship with those themes and their accompanying dilemmas in contemporary life, provide us with a renewed sense of wisdom and aesthetic vision for ministry and, indeed, a renewed wisdom about how life together should be lived. It can give depth and authority to the pastoral guidance we are to provide for God's people in our time. That authority will not be the authority of moralistic demand for conformity so much as it will be the authority of sound judgment and aesthetic vision.

Let us then turn first to an imaginative process of retrieval and historical-contemporary dialogue concerning the meaning of Christian presence in the world.

CHRISTIAN PRESENCE:
QUESTIONS AND VARIATIONS OF MEANING

What does it mean to be a Christian in the pluralistic world of the late twentieth century? Does identifying oneself as a Christian make any significant difference in how one is to be present in the world as we find it in our time? Or, said more aptly within the framework of understanding with which we have been working up to this point in this book, does the Christian tradition call forth from us a particular way of being in the world—a Christian presence?

If we reflect critically and carefully about that question, we are confronted at first not with an answer, but with a nest of further puzzling and difficult questions. What does it mean to be present? Is that something one can choose to do or not do? Is it a mode of being or is it a way of thinking about human being? Is it possible—or even desirable—to think about being a Christian as being *a* way of being present in the world? Would it not be better to think about a variety of ways of being present in the world, each of which has some identifiable rootage in traditional ways of thinking about being a Christian? Yet the question of truth and normativity keeps pressing itself upon us. What *should* it mean to be present in the world as the people of God who seek to follow the way of Christ?

So it is that thinking about the meaning of Christian presence in the world in which we find ourselves confronts us again with the reality of pluralism and the threat of fragmentation. It is not the case that pluralism and fragmentation are conditions out there in the world, while we who are Christians have a unity of being and purpose. Our common-sense desire that we could simply identify ourselves as Christians, and thus resolve our own struggle with the threat of fragmentation, runs up against the realization of the Christian community's age-old struggle to find unity of belief and practice in the midst of great diversity of understanding of what it means to be present in the world as Christians. We, as Christians, participate in the pluralism of our time.

It is well beyond the purpose of this writing to document fully the extent of the diversity among present-day Christians on the question of Christian presence in the world. It is nevertheless important to acknowledge that it is to a considerable degree because of the wide disparity of publicly visible models of Christian presence that the normative meaning of the presence of the people of God in the world has become problematic for many persons in contemporary Western society, both within and outside the self-identified Christian community. A quick impressionistic survey of some of those models will suffice to reveal the wide divergence that causes the voices of Christian presence to sound more like the dissonance of contemporary music than a unison chorus of the faithful.

In the so-called mainline Protestant churches, we see most prominently the results of the rise to dominance of the white middle class during the nineteenth and twentieth centuries, in which the meanings of Christian presence and white middle-class respectability became so fused to each other that the deeper biblical meanings of Christian presence in the world have tended to become obscured. Those middle-class ways of being Christian tended to emphasize class-oriented and male-dominated images of virility, independence, capitalistic boosterism, and gentility, such that Max Weber's "Protestant ethic and the spirit of capitalism" fulfilled itself in the dominant presence of middle-class Christian communities.[2] It was in all likelihood that set of images of Christian presence in the world that was predominant in the congregation Pastor Wall served in the case study discussed in the last chapter—a set of images intruded upon by the appearance of a black stranger in their midst.

In the early twentieth century and again as that century draws to a close, another closely related, but discordantly vocal, Christian perspective has made its presence known in American culture: the voice of fundamentalism and the religious right. Responding to this variation of the call to Christian presence in the world gives a peculiar twist to Protestant respectability involving a turn toward a stance of rigidity in matters as diverse as biblical inerrancy, condemnation of abortion and homosexuality, unquestioned patriotism, and compliance to specific preconceived formulas for the acceptance of Christian salvation. Spinning off from that mode of being present in contemporary culture are a number of variations, many of them made culturally highly visible by the hucksterism of their appropriation of television media. Taken together, these right-wing versions of Christian behavior have so confused the images of Christian presence as to make them unrecognizable or, worse, repugnant to many persons. Thus, they add to the fragmentation, rather than providing culturally viable responses to it in relation to the larger society.

As I said in the first chapter, no form of Christian presence in the contemporary world has had a greater transforming impact on American culture than has the presence of the black church. Because of its provision of a living, and unmistakably liberating, communal voice for justice and equity that refused not to be heard, the black church initiated a process of transformation within the society that is yet to realize its full potential. To it have been added a host of voices of liberation across the Third World and among women of virtually all nations, some—though not all—of whom claim a Christian origin for their presence in the world.

In these paragraphs, I have only begun to list the virtual cacophony of diverse voices that are being heard in the land, each claiming connections to Christian origins. To be sure, some make those claims with compelling conviction, while others seem only to acknowledge the claim with half-hearted or socially conformist self-identification. Nevertheless, each in one way or another claims a Christian presence. The question arises as to how such diversity can ever inform a new search for normative understanding of what it means to be present as the people of God in the world of the late twentieth century.

Is it not so, however, that from the beginning of Christian presence in the world, being a Christian has had a pluralism of meanings to different people? The writer of the Gospel of St. Matthew, for example, had very different notions about what it meant to be a follower of Christ than did the writer of Luke's Gospel. Paul and James certainly had differing ideas about that, as did, centuries later, their children in the faith, Martin Luther and John Calvin. Christian presence in the world has quite apparently never meant the same thing to all the great spokespersons for the faith, to say nothing of their more ordinary fellow travelers in the Way.[3]

To be reminded of the pluralism of Christian ways of being present in the worlds of the past can be salutary for those of us who are tempted to despair or cynicism about the disparity among the ways of Christian presence in our own time. It is to be reminded of the richness and variability of our tradition and thus to be invited to delve deeply into the stories and other historic texts of the Christian community in search not for the one ahistorical and forever true meaning of Christian presence, but for models from other ages that may have guidance to offer us in our struggle to be faithful in our time.

AN EXAMPLE OF THE AMBIGUITIES OF
CHRISTIAN PRESENCE TODAY

As proved to be the case in the previous two chapters, it may be that having before us a specific situation in which questions of Christian presence in the world are both hidden and predominant can assist us in probing beneath its cultural surface. I therefore want now to share in summary form a story that comes from a rather typical, in this case middle-class Protestant, congregation in a small American community in the mid-south. The story came to me through the participant observations of a young pastor who was serving his apprenticeship as pastoral assistant in the church, which understandably means that the happenings and characterizations in the story are colored somewhat by the teller's perspective. In order to protect the anonymity of the congregation and the pastoral author of the story, I will use fictitious names and include only those details that seem pertinent to my purpose here. Nevertheless, readers are asked to keep in mind that this is the story of an actual community and an actual set of circumstances.

The Smallberg United Protestant Church (actually a church affiliated with a mainline Protestant denomination) is a congregation of some nine hundred members who have recently moved to a new location and newly built sanctuary and educational building in an old, established county seat community of some twenty thousand people. The community has recently experienced some modest growth because of the location of several rather large industries on the outskirts of the town, at least one of which is related to the nuclear power industry. The church has thus also experienced some growth, a fact in part responsible for the decision to relocate the church from a down-town corner to the edge of one of the community's more affluent neighborhoods.

The Reverend Cone, the young assistant pastor from whom we hear the story of Smallberg U. P. Church, reports that, while the church has received many new members, the lay leadership of the congregation continues to be made up largely of long-time residents of the community and newcomers are generally seen as "outsiders in the local decision processes" of both the town and the church. Thus "lines of distinction between insider/outsider, North/South, white collar/blue collar, and black/white are still very evident."

The facility in which the congregation is now located is "the largest and most modern church in town. The cathedral style of architecture of the building made the transition into a higher order of liturgy more readily accepted." The changes have not been made without some resistance, however. "Some feel that the new building and higher liturgy has cost the church its friendly atmosphere." Membership, which was expected to grow rapidly, has leveled off and for the last few years has held steady, with additions coming mostly from the surrounding neighborhood. The physical attractiveness of the new location has apparently succeeded in drawing some people from the more affluent newcomers to the city, but it has failed to draw people from the entire town at the rate anticipated when the move from the downtown corner was decided upon.

The particular incident of Pastor Cone's story on which the action centers has to do with controversies that have arisen in relation to the church music program which, with the change in location and liturgical style, has become highly symbolic of the congregation's sense of its presence in the community. As might be expected, when the congregation moved to its new place of worship a new and more elaborately expensive organ was installed than the one that had been used for years in the old church. Pastor Cone reports that there are only three organists in the community capable of playing such a fine instrument, two of whom have long been employed by other congregations considered by Smallberg United Protestant congregants to be their "primary competitors" in the community.

The focal character in the present controversy in the church is Gene Oliver, the organist, a man considered by most of the musically informed church members to be by far the most talented musician in the community. Gene has had a long, if at times stormy, relationship with the Smallberg U. P. Church, although until recently he had not been a member of the church, but of another church in the community into which he had been baptized as a child. As a staff member of the church, Gene had been found to be not only a capable musician, but "a willing and supportive staff member, who was easy to work with." However, there were two clouds that hovered over Gene's relationship with the church: it was known that he had served a short prison sentence at some time in the past for writing bad checks, and he was thought by most of the church members to be homosexual. Despite these visible evidences of what were termed by many as "flaws in his character," Gene had many friends and supporters in the congregation, particularly among those who valued his musical talents.

Both these evidences of what some church members bluntly labeled Gene Oliver's sinfulness and others as his human frailty came sharply into public visibility within two years prior to Pastor Cone's telling of the story in a ministry theory seminar of which I was the leader. First, Gene was arrested for "propositioning" a young boy at a local shopping center. The story of his arrest was published in the Smallberg newspaper, together with the information that he was the organist at Smallberg U. P. Church: a public airing of "dirty linen" that many experienced as an "embarrassment to the church." A congregational personnel committee meeting was called and Gene was given "leave of absence from his organist duties while the legal proceedings took place." The charges of sexual molestation were nol-prossed with the understanding that Mr. Oliver would seek psychiatric counseling, an edict he complied with for a short time. At a subsequent meeting of the congregation's personnel committee, Gene appeared to be genuinely remorseful and asked the committee's forgiveness. The committee decided to accept these signs of repentance with the proviso of a "strong reprimand and warning about further embarrassment of the church." As one member put it, "Gene, anyone can make a mistake, but if we have another problem of any kind, even a traffic violation, I'll be the first to recommend your dismissal."

Action of the personnel committee did not, however, end the controversy. Vocal criticism of the committee and the pastoral leaders continued to be heard from both moralistically conservative parishioners and some denominational officials. Somewhat to the surprise or even dismay of some, it was at this point that Gene Oliver asked for and, after due consideration by congregational leaders, received membership in the church.

Unfortunately, less than a year after the apparent resolution of the charges of homosexual impropriety, Mr. Oliver was again arrested, this time on a charge of embezzlement of funds from the payroll department of his employer, a plant with contracts with the U.S. government. It happened that the elected lay leader of the congregation was the chief operating officer of the plant where Gene was employed as an accountant. He testified in court against Mr. Oliver, who was then sentenced to a three-year prison term, one year of which was to be actually served at the state penitentiary, with the other two served on probation. Gene Oliver went to prison. While there, he has been visited regularly by Pastor Cone and, on occasion, by various members of the congregation.

In Gene's absence, a substitute organist from a community at some fifty miles distance from Smallberg has been employed on a temporary basis by the church personnel committee. Her talents, while not woefully lacking, fall far short of the standard to which Mr. Oliver's abilities had accustomed the congregation. Many, particularly among the musically inclined, began to express their anticipation of Gene's return. Others were vehemently vocal in their opposition to having their music provided by a "known homosexual embezzler." As the time approached for Gene Oliver's parole, the controversy has begun to become heated to the point of threatening the already fragile unity of the church. According to Pastor Cone, the two ordained leaders of the congregation are themselves at odds over the issue, Cone himself taking the position that "the community of faith should be a community embodying forgiveness and grace," while the senior pastor has spoken of "taking a moral stand against unacceptable behavior." Cone suspects that the senior pastor is also concerned about declining financial commitments to the church, and the still large indebtedness acquired in the construction of the new physical plant.

The attitudes expressed by congregants reflect in part the same divisions of opinion of their ordained leaders. However, some, according to Pastor Cone, are primarily interested in restoring the quality of musical support of Sunday morning worship. These people tend to say things on the order of "Gene is not really a bad person. In fact, he is a very good person who happens to have some minor and ordinary human problems." The plant superintendent lay leader, on the other hand, vigorously supports the position of the senior minister and says it would be "immoral" for the church to reinstate Gene as organist.

At the time of Pastor Cone's telling of the story, the situation in Smallberg United Protestant Church remains unresolved and very much in doubt. Pastor Cone is thinking about transferring to another congregation because he feels powerless to bring about the resolution to the controversy that he feels would express Christian norms for responding to such situations, and thus make a "Christian statement" about the faith community's presence in the town. The senior pastor, on the other hand, is worried about deepening divisions in his flock and about church finances. Gene Oliver awaits his parole and hopes for return to the Smallberg U. P. organ loft. The townspeople look on curiously to see how this small segment of the people of God will resolve their dilemma.

THE SMALLBERG CONGREGATION'S PRESENCE IN ITS WORLD

Particularly if we are accustomed to thinking about such problems as that in the Smallberg congregation in moralistic terms, our first impulse might tend to be to focus on the making of the right decision by the congregation. However, the approach taken in the earlier chapters of this book suggests taking a somewhat different tack. Pursuing the imaginative, metaphorical, aesthetic mode of reflection with which we are working in this book, I suggest that we first inquire about what appears when we look at this relatively ordinary story of a church controversy through the lens of the metaphor of presence. In softly focused perspective, first, how is this congregation as a community seeking to be present in the world of its time and place? By what actions and decisions has and is that presence making itself known in visible ways that, with or without the congregation's being self-aware and intentional, speak of its vision of what it means to be the people of God in the world?

The first thing that comes to mind is that the church has recently moved its visible symbol of its presence from a busy street corner in the center of the town's public activity to a more private and aesthetically pleasant location. Its relocation appears to be from a public to a private symbolic visibility. Is it not possible that this physical relocation symbolizes a movement away from a vision of Christian presence that draws to itself the flow of public issues and problems of a larger human community toward a more sequestered, privatized location that draws to itself the concerns of an affluent community for its own comfort and pleasure? Unacknowledged in the stated hopes for the move (that the larger, more aesthetically pleasing buildings and location would attract people from all

100

across the town), that subtle, but commonly held, vision of what Christian presence can and should mean is now fulfilling itself in several thought-provoking and unexpected ways. The new people who are now being attracted to the church do not come from all social levels and classes of the community, but only from those who live in the comfort of the affluent neighborhood. The race and class barriers of the community, rather than having been broken through, have in subtle and insidious ways been exacerbated. To the congregational leaders' dismay, the church is not growing larger and more significant for the entire town, but is becoming more insulated!

At a somewhat different, but related level, it is a bit disturbing to note that for some in the congregation an overriding criterion that seems now to identify the presence of this people of God in their community has become the pleasing sound issuing forth from the church organ while the people of God are at worship—a sound that must at all costs be as artistically beautiful as the sounds made by organists in "competing" centers of worship in the town! In unexpected ways, almost as if planned by a cunning Madison Avenue commercial product promoter, the competitive vision of American success in business life has crept into the metaphorical images the move to the new sanctuary has produced.

It is also provocative of significant theological reflection to note that the move of the congregation toward privatization of their presence in the community has not proven entirely successful. Their escape from the issues of the world into the beauty and tranquility of their new location has, despite the hidden intention of their actions, been interrupted in a quite unexpected way. Three issues of public life in America that have drawn increasing attention in the public press—homosexuality, child sexual abuse, and white collar crime—have intruded themselves on the quiet comfort of the new location in the person of the church organist! The question as to how they are to be present in the world in relation to these three matters of public concern has been thrust upon them in a manner that makes the issues inescapable. The issues of the street corner are now in their organ loft!

PASTORAL PRESENCE IN THE SMALLBERG SITUATION

Leaving these reflections on the Smallberg congregational presence in its world for the moment, I suggest we now look at the behavior and concerns of the ordained leaders of the congregation through the metaphorical lens of presence. In inquiring into the expression of their

101

ministry by means of the metaphor of presence, we are taking up a theme that has become—in certain restricted ways—standard within the pastoral care literature of recent decades. That literature, particularly as it has formulated a pastoral theology of crisis ministry, has made significant use of the metaphor of presence. It has, therefore, become commonplace to think in terms of the symbolic meaning of pastoral presence in human situations of need, most particularly those situations in which communication through spoken language is difficult. In hermeneutically oriented pastoral theologies, pastoral presence has come to be seen as enacting or opening up a "world of meaning."[4]

How are these two pastors being present in the situation in which they find themselves, and what do their quite apparently different ways of being present seem to convey as to the meaning of Christian presence? What can we extrapolate from the story Pastor Cone tells about the visions of ministry and of Christian presence in the world that are informing the ways in which they are being ministers of Christ in the situation confronting Smallberg U. P. Church? What are the evidences, if any, of their exercise of wise judgment?

Since he is the teller of the Smallberg story, let us look first at Pastor Cone's manner of being present in the situation. The first thing we note is that Pastor Cone appears to identify himself with Gene Oliver, the organist and breaker of the community's accepted norms. His first concern appears to be that Mr. Oliver receive the forgiveness and acceptance of the congregation—forgiveness and acceptance that he not only needs, but also that are due him as a sinner in need of grace. It is Pastor Cone who has most faithfully visited Gene during his stay in the penitentiary: visits that, from the manner in which Pastor Cone tells of them, we can imagine were designed primarily to communicate to Gene that he had not been forgotten or rejected as a result of his conviction and imprisonment.

We find ourselves wishing that Pastor Cone had included more details in his story concerning the nature of those visits with Gene Oliver. What did they talk about? Gene's loneliness and fearful isolation in prison? His struggle with his homosexuality: a struggle undoubtedly exacerbated by imprisonment in an all-male population? His guilt and remorse over his thievery? His puzzlement at his own behavior? His need and desire for God's forgiveness? We do not know. What we do know is that, as he anticipates Oliver's return to the community, Pastor Cone is preoccupied with the question of congregational expression of acceptance and grace. His primary concern seems not to be with possible moral issues for either the congregation or Gene Oliver. His vision of Christian ministry and presence does not appear to give these matters high priority. His choice is rather to be graciously present with the individual who has offended the community's standards.[5]

Further reflection on Pastor Cone's manner of being present in the situation soon brings to our attention a certain quality of passivity and powerlessness in his manner of telling the story. Cone does not come forth as a strong or determined actor in the situation. His stance is rather that of the participant-observer. He seems to be keeping to himself whatever wisdom he has to offer in the situation. Furthermore, rather than sharing his thoughts about what he—as one of the ministers—can do to help redeem the situation, he speaks of his desire to withdraw from it and look elsewhere to fulfill his ministry. One wonders why that is the case? Does it simply have to do with being young and in a secondary status as the assistant pastor of the church? Or is there a possible connection between his passivity in his vision of his present ministry and his manner of identifying with Gene Oliver as the one in need of grace, rather than the one with a certain level of responsibility for taking hold of his life and situation? We cannot be sure, but it does seem apparent that Pastor Cone has either consciously or unconsciously decided to allow his presence to be that of the passive observer and critic.

The story, as Pastor Cone tells it, gives us only a few specific clues with which to reflect on the senior pastor's presence in the Smallberg situation. We do get the clear impression that he played a major role in the congregation's decision to relocate. He seems clearly to have made a considerable investment in helping to shape the cathedral-like style of architecture and the higher liturgical style of worship that has developed in the new location. Furthermore, he has apparently encouraged the lay leadership, through its appropriate committee, to take responsibility for the congregation's management of the problems with Gene Oliver. We are told that, like his lay leader, he opposes the reemployment of Mr. Oliver as organist on moral grounds. He is now worried about finances and about the divisions he fears are developing in the congregation as a result of the organist controversy.

Nowhere, on the other hand, does Pastor Cone's story tell us about the senior pastor's efforts to confront the societal, ethical, and theological ambiguities and issues that are hidden in the congregation's situation. We are not, for example, provided with any information concerning his relationship and possible discussions with the music lovers of the congregation who, for their own private aesthetic reasons, take what seems to the outside observer a fatuously sentimental stance toward Gene Oliver's problems. The story does not tell us anything about his efforts to minister to Gene Oliver. Rather, it would appear that, having decided that Oliver's past behavior is morally reprehensible, he now supports breaking off the congregation's relationship with him—at least insofar as it involves his possible return to the role of church organist. The primary focus of his presence in the situation seems to be as institutional administrator with overriding concern for organizational integrity and finances. We must, however, acknowledge an ambiguity. The senior minister did stand with his personnel committee in retaining Mr. Oliver after the incident of homosexual child abuse, even at the cost of strong criticism from some of the laity and denominational officials. There is no evidence that he has or wants to reject Gene Oliver as a member of the congregation. The primary question concerning his presence in the situation is whether or not he is prepared to give wise leadership that cuts beneath or moves beyond organizational concerns.

In summary, it would appear that the aesthetic visions informing the stances and actions of the two pastoral figures in the Smallberg situation not only differ in significant respects, but also remain ambiguous. Whatever wisdom is orienting the pastoral guidance being offered, the Smallberg congregation seems fragmented and lacking a well articulated, historically-informed theology of the church. The question of what images of presence of both pastoral leaders and congregation is most fitting for their situation cries out for clarification.

THE PRESENCE OF GENE OLIVER

We cannot leave our reflections on the Smallberg situation without giving some imaginative attention to the shape and power of Gene Oliver's presence on the scene in Smallberg U. P. Church. His presence is indeed the most powerful of all. Oliver's presence cuts through the veneer of privatistic respectability covering the outward manifestations of Smallberg's aesthetic vision of itself to expose deep and disturbing human flaws, not only in his own make-up and behavior, but in the congregation's aesthetic vision of itself. His presence comes to the Smallberg congregation as a powerful reminder of twisted human desire and contradiction. Gene Oliver's presence has been exposed to reveal a radically inconsistent mixture of talents and sinfulness. Though they may not all recognize it as such, for the congregation that means that the prettily decorated facade-like presence of this people is exposed as harboring not only wrongdoing, but unmet human needs and faulty human maturation. The presence of Gene Oliver confronts the Smallberg people with the reality that attempting to live as the people of God involves deeper and more crucial issues than beautifully decorated sanctuaries and artistically correct music. Indeed, his presence has thrust the congregation out of its sanctuary and into the streets and dirty back alleys of the human predicament.

Reflecting on the presence of Gene Oliver in these terms, I cannot resist wondering if his presence in the situation does not harbor a redemptive possibility. The intrusion of his abberant behavior has certainly stirred the congregation out of its privatistic complacency. Suddenly, there are issues to be discussed that truly matter and have public importance involving good and evil. Issues have arisen that demand the exercise of sound judgment and actions that express a fundamental wisdom about human affairs. The basic question of what it means to be a community concerned with human sin and salvation has unmistakably appeared in the community's midst. Age-old questions about the interrelationship of law and gospel have been made concrete and particular.

The question as to how Gene Oliver is attempting to be present in the Smallberg faith community, however, raises questions of a somewhat different order. Perusing Pastor Cone's story, I am struck, as I was in my reflections on Cone's presence, with the aura of passivity that surrounds Oliver's persona. Following his arrest on the sexual charge, he asks to be given membership in the congregation. Now he awaits the congregation's acceptance back into his old position. He seems somehow reluctant to take an active stance of responsibility for his actions and make appropriate amends for his behavior. Within the language of psychological interpretation, this passivity in his intentional presence can be interpreted as further evidence of his faulty development. But within Christian ways of speaking about repentance and responsible search for new beginnings, we are impressed with a recognizable reluctance to step forward and seek reconciliation with the community of the faithful. Rather, Gene Oliver simply waits.

RETRIEVING A NORMATIVE VISION OF CHRISTIAN PRESENCE

Up to this point, our reflections on the Smallberg United Protestant congregation's situation through the imaginative metaphor of presence have been largely phenomenological and descriptive. We have thereby uncovered significant ways in which both the presence of the congregation in its community and the presence of three key individuals in the situation confronting the church are strongly colored by unacknowledged—or only implicitly articulate—visions concerning the normative meaning of Christian presence in the world. At this point, our inquiry needs therefore to turn toward an effort to recover the deep wisdom of the Judeo-Christian tradition concerning the presence of God's people in the world. Our search is for a normative vision of Christian presence that will both fit the Smallberg situation *and* constitute fitting wisdom with roots deep in the historic community with which the Smallberg church identifies itself.

We turn here quite instinctively to the Bible as the Christian community's primordial source for normative images of Christian presence in the world. This is particularly the case for Protestant Christians who, from the time of the Reformation, have been a "People of the Book." It is the Bible that contains the storied texts that tell the people of God who they are in their deepest origins and what their presence in the world signifies. Rich and varied as those storied texts are by virtue of the long reach of biblical time with the shifting circumstances surrounding and confronting God's people across the centuries from Genesis to Revelation, do they provide us with anything that could be called a unified aesthetic vision of what it normatively means to be present in the world as the people of God? Failing that, are there themes concerning presence that appear and reappear amidst the changes of time and circumstance, and thus provide a thread that identifies the continuing conversation of God's people concerning the meaning of their presence in the world?

In a powerfully illuminating book with the provocative title *The Elusive Presence* by the highly respected biblical scholar Samuel Terrien, the theme of presence is traced as an organizing metaphor across the long sweep of biblical history.[6] In his book, Terrien argues that the significance of the metaphor of presence is primary in biblical religion, even more primary than the metaphor of covenant, which is so important for Old Testament understanding of the human-God relationship. Furthermore, it was "a new theology of presence, drawn from the Hebraic complex of cultus and faith, which presided over the emergence of Christianity from Judaism."[7]

The presence metaphor, as Terrien traces it, has first to do with the Israelite sensitivity to the presence of God. In the early stories reported in Genesis, God's presence, which was spoken of in very concrete and down-to-earth ways through such images as that of God "walking in the garden in the cool of the day" and speaking in human tongue out of bushes that burned without being consumed—ways that may seem primatively childlike to sophisticated moderns, began the shaping of a theology that was unique in the world of antiquity.

> The cults of antiquity offer many close parallels to the religion of Israel, but a basic difference stands out between them. The epiphanies of the gods of the

106

ancient Near East and in classical antiquity imply a deification of the forces of nature, of human desires, of tribal or national needs for economic survival and political stability, and of the dynastic drive for imperial conquest. Such a process appears in Mesopotamia, in Egypt, in Syria-Phoenicia-Canaan, in Iran, and later in Greece and Rome. Cosmogonies were in effect theogonies and therefore suggested the finite character of the godhead. Either the gods and goddesses did not transcend the temporality of the natural forces or else they were identified with a universe viewed as eternal. The pluralism of the deities reveals a fragmentariness of the prevailing world views or appears to have been related to some form of determinism to which the gods themselves were subject.

In Israel, on the contrary, while anthropocentric concerns were not altogether absent, natural space and historical time remained utterly dependent upon a free sovereign, whose transcendence was never divorced from a "pathetic" concern for the welfare of human and even animal life. The knowledge of this free and sovereign God informs Israel's standard of faith. It promotes her ideal of peoplehood and is the main source of her ethics. Such knowledge stems from a single factor: the Hebraic theology of presence.[8]

Terrien makes clear two highly determinative things concerning the image of presence in Hebrew experience. First, the image of presence originally had to do with the reality and character of Yahweh's presence. Yahweh became to the Hebrew people a sovereign and independent deity whose transcendence was never divorced from the pathos of Yahweh's concern for human welfare. Second, the meaning of the presence of the Israelite people as the people of God found its origins in their perceptions of God's presence among them and in their world. The qualities that were to characterize the presence of God's people were the qualities that characterized God's concern for human well-being.

Several things stand out in Terrien's further development of the metaphor of presence in relation to God and the Hebrew people. First, he underlines the fact that biblical Hebrew "did not apparently possess an abstract word meaning 'presence.'" That being the case, they turned to human metaphors as a way of speaking about the elusive presence of Yahweh.[9] The human face, so important in the visual awareness of another human being, became a metaphor for the immediate and intimate presence of God. God "showed himself." (Note in that expression a double human metaphor. God, like a person "shows" or "does not show" God's self. The chosen human metaphor is also masculine, after the manner of Hebrew masculine patriarchy.) In the stories of Yahweh's appearances, metaphors of human walking and talking, coming and going are used. As with humans, God is either present or absent, and God's coming is to be sought and awaited. More often than not, God is simply heard rather than seen, and to hear God's voice, the human ear must be sensitively attuned to hear. Thus, from very early, Hebrew faith took on an eschatological aura of anticipation.[10]

Second, from very early in the development of Hebrew worship of Yahweh, an awareness took form that Yahweh's presence or absence, speaking or silence, was elusively beyond human control. God's ways were God's and they must be accepted, and an understanding of them sought in humility and faith, rather than their being directed or evoked by human desire. Furthermore, God, in ways metaphorically analogous to humans, was capable of wrath as well as gentleness, was jealous of God's primacy and thus countenanced "no other gods before me." Discerning the intentions of God in history, the presence or absence of God's activity in the affairs of human beings became a dominant motif in Hebrew religious life.

> Israel rose to a sublimity of theological perception because she understood the paradox of presence in absence. She knew that God hidden is still God. She served a God who forsook her and even stood up against her as an enemy in order to teach her the selflessness of devotion. Grace in God means gratuitous love in man. Intimacy between God and Israel is secure.[11]

There are, to be sure, inconsistencies evident in the long history of Israelite religion with regard to human control and access to the presence of God. The narratives of both the Ark of the Covenant that was carried to and fro across the countryside by a nomadic people, and of the building, destruction, and rebuilding of the Temple in Jerusalem tell of the desire of the Israelite community to locate access to God in a particular place and ritual observance. In the eras of the kings of Israel, efforts were made to identify the presence and purposes of God with the presence and purposes of earthly monarchs of power. But even in those narratives, the elusiveness of God's presence or absence to which the people were simply subject is in large part preserved.[12]

Third, the Hebrew understanding of divine presence in the world and divine purpose in the Israelite community greatly enlarged and directed their understanding of their individual and collective presence in the wider world of human affairs. From the time when Abraham received a blessing from God, the Israelite mission in the world came to "be a blessing" (Gen. 12:2) to all the peoples of the earth. As their God was a universal God with the welfare of all humankind as the scope of godly concern, so the people of God were to be a blessing and source of reconciliation for all the nations. They were to be interested not only in their own welfare, but also in the welfare of all. Thus, metaphors of openness to the stranger, concern for the least and last, such as the widow and the orphan, that is, justice and equity in all human affairs, entered into the self-understanding of the Old Testament people of God. The long story of the rise and fall of the Hebrew people is to a considerable degree the story of the appearance and disappearance from time to time and situation to situation of those motifs of universalism, justice, and reconciliation.[13]

With the coming of the time told about in the narratives of the Gospels, a new and culminating recognition of the presence of God in the midst of human affairs took hold among those who became the first Christians. The elusive presence of God became tangible in the presence of Jesus. He became for his followers not only the embodiment of the qualities of godly presence, but also a model to be emulated in the presence of God's people in the world.

> For such a people of God, in the world not for themselves but for the reconciliation of all humans with God and for the mending of the entire fallen creation, Jesus had poignant images. All of them pointed to the new sense of fellowship, in which the disciples were freed from worldly concerns with proprietorship and control to live in the new eschatological reality: The Kingdom was present like leaven in the dough, quietly bringing about the good for the whole loaf. It was like the mustard seed, tiny, but containing a surprising potential. The disciples were to be the salt of the earth not there to transform everything else into salt, but there for the health of all. They were to be a lamp held high, present in the world for God's glory.[14]

Vivid and compelling as were these earthy metaphors for Christian presence Jesus provided in his sayings, they were made even more transforming by the power of the image of Jesus as the incarnate presence of God with us. In the narratives of the crucified and resurrected Jesus, the people of God found their assurance of God's suffering, redeeming, continuing presence in the world.

The contemporary German theologian Jürgen Moltmann, in making the turn away from traditional Christian theology's preoccupation with images of power and *apatheia* in relation to God toward images of *pathos* and suffering, writes:

> The incarnate God is present, and can be experienced, in the humanity of every [person], and in full human corporeality. No one need dissemble and appear other than he [or she] is to perceive the fellowship of the human God with him [or her]. Rather, he [or she] can lay aside all dissembling and sham and become what [one] truly is in this human God. Furthermore, the crucified God is near to [persons] in the forsakenness of every [person].

There is no loneliness and no rejection which he has not taken to himself and assumed in the cross of Jesus. There is no need for any attempts at justification or for any self-destructive self-accusations to draw near to him. . . . [Humanity is] taken up, without limitations and conditions, into the life and suffering, the death and resurrection of God, and in faith participates corporeally in the fullness of God. There is nothing that can exclude [them] from the situation of God between the grief of the Father, the love of the Son and the drive of the Spirit.[15]

Thus, to be present in the world as one, or as a community of God's people, is to participate in the life and promises of God. It is to take upon oneself or one's community the burden and the calling of God's suffering, patient, mysteriously active movement to transform all creation into the Kingdom of God's rule of justice, equity, and abundant fulfillment of the promises and purposes hidden in creation. It is to do and be what is fitting for the fulfillment of those promises and purposes.

SMALLBERG REVISITED

Upon returning to the story of Smallberg United Protestant Church from this all too brief and sketchy journey of retrieval into the biblical narrative sources that tell of the origins of Christian understanding of divine and human presence in the world, I am struck by the manner in which, in Smallberg, certain twentieth-century ways of thinking about and evaluating human presence have obscured the deeper originating wisdom of our tradition. The common sense of the people, both leaders and lay people in the congregation, seems somehow impoverished of so much of the metaphorical richness of their origins. Where, for example, are the images that tie together an acute sensitivity to the presence of God in the life of the people and images of who the people of God are to be? Not only does God seem no longer metaphorically to walk in the gardens of Smallberg, but one is hard pressed to hear any indication of human desire to know what God is interested in bringing about in the complexities and controversies of the situation now being confronted by God's people.

What is much more evident is the expressed concern for such things as the success or failure of the congregation's move to its new quarters and location, the outbreak of controversy over the morality or immorality of harboring a known homosexual with a prison record in the sanctuary, and the ability or inability of the congregation to offer acceptance to a publicly identified sinner. Each of those issues, when seen afresh after delving into primal biblical images, is revealed as being given interpretive understanding through images and themes devoid of much of the richness of biblical metaphors concerning divine and human presence. On the other hand, certain twentieth-century images and themes are, as I indicated in the earlier discussion of the case, very much in evidence. They are the themes of propriety, morality, public image or appearance, and competitive success or failure.

Yet, one can detect certain traces of a vision of the deeper metaphorical wisdom of the community rooted in the stories of the Bible. The taking of Gene Oliver into membership at the time of public exposure of his homosexuality sounds echoes of the biblical theme of welcoming the stranger, and perhaps of concern for the oppressed and rejected of the world. More recently, the controversy over what should be the church's relationship to Gene upon his return from prison harbors traces of those same metaphorical themes. So also does Pastor Cone's concern with acceptance and forgiveness of Gene by the congregation and its leaders. Even the moralistic stance of the senior pastoral and lay leaders contains a kernel of the biblical community's dialectical efforts to balance law with compassion and mercy.

One thing that is both qualitatively and quantitatively missing from the Smallberg story is sufficient evidence of the appropriation of a rich grammar of imagistic wisdom sufficiently varied and subtle in its implications to allow an aesthetically normative inquiry to take place among members of the community. Without that imagistic language, the people are greatly limited in their abilities to carry on an inquiring conversation that may lead in the direction of solutions to the problematic issues of the situation that are fitting, given who the people of the Smallberg congregation identify themselves as being. Without that language, their controversial debates, and even their private ruminations over the problems at hand, are constricted and unimaginative. They become, as was discussed in chapter 3, subject simply to the rule of common sense, whether that be the common sense of moralistic judgmentalism or the overly simplistic common-sense notion that Christians should be accepting and forgiving.

The contemporary process theologian John B. Cobb, Jr., in a brief but thoughtful book entitled *Theology and Pastoral Care*, speaks cogently of this problem of the poverty of contemporary religious language bereft of biblical imagery. Cobb asserts that "if the church is to regain health it must recover the ability to use historic Christian imagery and rhetoric with power and authenticity."[16] But, says Cobb, the regaining of imaginative contact with biblical language and imagery is not an easy or simple one.

He suggests that, because the language and imagery of the Bible tends to be strange and archaic to persons shaped by the language and imagery of the contemporary world, our first response is to "find equivalents in contemporary idiom." He uses the biblical word *sin* as an example. Our inclination is to find equivalents in contemporary words such as *alienation, defensiveness,* and *closedness.* "Perhaps then we can decide that the meaning of *sin* in the Bible is the same as what is meant by *alienation* or *defensiveness* or *closedness* today. With such an understanding we can once again use the word *sin.*"

But, says Cobb, that is not really a satisfactory solution.

> The word *sin* in the Bible has its own integrity of meaning interconnected with the meanings of other biblical words. For example, it carried the note of personal and corporate responsibility without reducing the context to a moral one. It lifted to consciousness in the community in which it was used, dimensions of experience that are not the same as those elicited by our modern words. Thus it contributed to a world of meaning that is different from the dominant ones of our time. To translate the words of that different world into our language makes them meaningful to us, but it does so by denying them their own meanings.[17]

Cobb acknowledges that this radical difference between the world of images and meanings of the Bible and the language and meaning world of contemporary life presents a difficult dilemma for the church and for ministry. If we only translate biblical images and meanings into a contemporary idiom—what we already know—then the imagistic meaning world of the Bible is rendered powerless to speak to us with the authority of a perspective other than the surrounding contemporary culture. Yet, those biblical images and themes must be brought into active and rich dialogue with contemporary life if we are to be true to our grounding identity as the people of God who claim the biblical record as the record of our origins.

What, therefore, is needed most urgently in the community of God's people is the engendering of a richly imaginative and continuing conversation that seeks to bring together in dialogue the meanings, images, and themes of the historic biblical community in its full sweep across biblical history, on the one hand, and the images, themes, and situational dilemmas of contemporary life, on the other hand, so that those two differing but deeply related horizons may speak to each other. Only then can the common sense vision of what it means to be present in the world as the people of God that is prevalent in countless contemporary congregations as it appears to be in the Smallberg church be enriched, enlivened, and, yes, brought under judgment by the deep and primal wisdom of the tradition by which our churches are named. It is just such a lively and richly imaginative dialogue that seems clearly to be missing in the story of the Smallberg church and its situation of conflict.[18] Such a dialogical process may not provide simple, direct, and explicit answers to questions about what morally ought to be done in Smallberg Church in regard to Gene Oliver, but it can engender an ethos of inquiry that can enlarge and enlighten the Smallberg congregation's understanding of its situation and its vision of what its Christian presence demands.

The second thing missing in the Smallberg story is adequate evidence that the congregation or its leaders are giving sufficient attention to questions concerning the presence of God in the situation at hand. What, given the situation as it exists, is God seeking to bring about? Are there any signs of God's redeeming, creative, transforming presence? As we found in our retrieval of Hebrew imagistic ways of defining the purpose and intention of God's people by means of discerning the purpose and intention of God, is it possible imaginatively to discern what the Smallberg people of God are called to be in their situation by means of reflection on questions of the presence or absence of God, God's intentions, God's speaking or God's silence, God's transformative desire? Is God to be found only in the private seclusion of the new sanctuary and the beauty of the service of worship? On the other hand, is God with the ones who are missing from the congregation now that they have moved to the location of affluence? Is God acting in the person of Gene Oliver to bring forcibly before the congregation the necessity that they confront the public issues of the day? What is God seeking to bring about?

PASTORAL PRESENCE AND PASTORAL CARE

At this point, I can hear readers turning quite naturally and instinctively to thoughts about what needs to be said by the Smallberg pastors from the pulpit of the new sanctuary. (And, parenthetically, we need to acknowledge that Pastor Cone, in telling the story, has said nothing about what was being said from that pulpit! More may have been going on there by way of confronting the issues of the situation than is apparent from the telling of the story.) I am reminded that in the twentieth-century models of ministry, the place and time at which biblical metaphors, images, and themes are most often expected to be heard is during the sermon at the eleven o'clock hour on Sunday morning. Biblical language is supposed to be the language of the pulpit.

But what of biblical imagery and its use in the ministry of pastoral care? Here, perhaps except in the case of pastoral care ministry to the sick, the dying, and the bereaved, biblical imagery has by and large disappeared. The grammar of pastoral care has become, for the most part, the grammar of contemporary psychological and relational language. In the phrase of the American church historian, E. Brooks Holifield, the language of salvation has been replaced by the language of self-realization.[19] Within that process, something quite analogous to what John Cobb found to be the case with contemporizations of the concept of sin has taken place. Such metaphors as growth, becoming, self-fulfillment, empathy, and autonomy in relationships have become popular as present-day equivalents to such biblical imagery as abundant life, righteousness, and compassion. Even though these contemporary, largely psychologized images have served a useful purpose in relating the knowledge and dynamic meanings of modern psychology to pastoral work, when used as equivalents to biblical imagery, they rob pastoral conversations of much of the deep metaphorical wisdom of the biblical tradition.

One of the puzzling, unforeseen, and unfortunate consequences of the psychologizing of pastoral care language and imagery has been the frequently observed pastoral discomfiture with the use of Christian and biblical language in pastoral care conversations. Pastors who do not hesitate to use biblical metaphors and images in the pulpit will often become embarrassed and awkward in the use of these metaphors in private conversations with parishioners seeking guidance concerning a variety of human relational problems. Devoid of such images, pastoral presence in relationships of care is in danger of becoming presence indistinguishable from the presence of any other psychologically-minded counselor. Such modes of pastoral presence are thereby impoverished of that aesthetic wisdom that can facilitate the restoration of Christian presence in all circumstances of life together to a deep and informing continuity with Christian origins.

It must also be said, however, that pastoral care ministry that consists simply in the mouthing of biblical language in a heavy-handed effort to reduce the complexities of such human situations as that involving Gene Oliver and the Smallberg congregation to some supposed biblical simplicity will likewise fall far short of the metaphorical wisdom in the contemporary situation for which we seek. Such wisdom will only emerge from a process of profound search for both the significance of the ever-changing situational circumstances that make up the flow of life in the present *and* for the critical perspectives on those circumstances that the otherness of biblical metaphors can provide. It is just such dialogical inquiry that is demanded of the contemporary pastor in all of the caring relationships of pastoral work. And it is such dialogical inquiry that the pastor should invite from those of his or her parishioners who would seek to be present in the world of their day-to-day relationships as the people of God.

CHAPTER FIVE

NORMATIVE METAPHORS FOR PASTORAL WORK:

Community

I n his somewhat turgid but profoundly moving play, *Joe Turner's Come and Gone*, Pulitzer prize-winning African-American playwright August Wilson develops a theme that is echoed throughout late twentieth century American culture: The theme of wistful longing for community, the counterpoint to the age of the self. Wilson sets his development of that theme in what must appear to many in the dominant white middle-class culture of American affluence as an unexpected context—an appearance that may account for the fact that the play, while receiving virtually unanimous critical acclaim, had only a short run in the New York mecca of American theater. The play is about poor rural blacks who, shortly after the turn of the century, fled the cotton plantations of the American South to seek a better life in the industrial cities of the Northeast. Economically marginal, fundamentally homeless, each quite apparently in search of someone or something lost and longed for, the play's characters are drawn to a run-down Pittsburgh rooming house seeking temporary shelter. Thrown together, they play out their woeful but powerfully dramatic search for a community of kindred spirits. Temporarily, ephemerally, they find it, largely thanks to the ministrations of an ignorantly wise and sensitive conjurman who claims a mysterious power to "bind folks together that ought to be bound."

Although much of the power of August Wilson's play emerges from his ability to portray the sensibilities of displaced poor black people newly escaped from the bondage of white-dominated Southern near-slavery into the empty freedom of urban lower-class life, the play also resonates metaphorically with both the bondages and longings of many in mainstream America who likewise feel strangely displaced and in search of something they feel they have lost. It resonates, peculiarly, with the

116

sensibility of the business executive whose sense of dismay and homelessness began our reflections on the development of the threat of normlessness in chapter 1. Distant and different in time and place location as my six-figured income businessman friend may seem on the surface to be from Wilson's characters, at the level of their deepest fears and desires, they are kinfolk in important respects.

The theme of search for community is present as well in the other vignettes of human interaction with which we have worked in earlier chapters of this book. It is a primary theme in the story of the street parking controversy in chapter 2. It is central to the story of Pastor Wall's prophetic ministry to his congregation as they reluctantly expanded the boundaries of their church community to include a stranger of another race. In a more problematic sense, the theme of community can be seen as a crucial but hidden theme in the story of Smallberg United Protestant Church in the previous chapter.

My thesis, that the search for community is increasingly difficult, will not be heard as new or surprising to readers who are in touch with current commentary about American society. Indeed, the word *community* threatens to become a mere buzzword tossed about by one and all. Readers may, therefore, justifiably ask what there is left to say about it that can add anything significant to the literal flood of conversation and commentary the catchword has gathered around it in recent times.

The theme of community must be included as a normative metaphorical theme, not simply because it gathers to itself many of the frustrated longings of this time in American life experience, but because it is a theme that, when properly understood, likewise gathers to itself much of the deepest wisdom of the Judeo-Christian tradition. As such, it is a metaphor that can critically inform the work of ministry in relation to the recovery of and search for norms, boundaries, and visions of the good life. Not only that, it is a metaphorical lens through which may be revealed a number of the more significant ways in which twentieth-century life in its common sense forms has lost touch with the deep wisdom of the biblical tradition. If that be the case, then its pertinence for ministry in late twentieth-century America becomes apparent. Just how that pertinence for pastoral practice becomes operationally normative will comprise the work of the remaining pages of this chapter.

PASTORAL WORK AND THE SEARCH FOR COMMUNITY

For the parish pastor, no matter where her or his parish may be located, the task of nurturing and sustaining a viable community of believers is a constant and multifaceted one. It provides a primary measure of the success or failure of the minister's effort to nurture a unity of belief and practice among the diverse people of a congregation. It is the measure by which individual parishioners most often assess the viability of their relationship to their local church. It is encountered whenever the pastor visits in the homes of prospective members of the congregation. Inviting persons into membership in the church necessarily involves facilitating a process whereby persons who have been strangers in search of a religious community move toward becoming "at home" with fellow Christians—at home both in the sense of having found a place where their religious needs and desires may be focused, and in the sense of having found a network of human relationships in which they feel secure and valued. Increasingly, particularly in the urban context of high mobility and anonymity, the ties that bind a religious community to a place and a sustained and sustaining relational network can tend to become more tenuous and fragile. Personally and programmatically nurturing and strengthening those ties are central to the role of the parish pastor.

COMMON-SENSE NOTIONS OF THE CHURCH AND MINISTRY

It is just at this point that, upon reflection, we become aware of ways in which certain common-sense notions—notions gradually developed over time in the American cultural location to the point of being taken for granted—concerning both pastoral role and the sustaining structure of a religious relational community have become dominant in the American churches. My contention is that this taken-for-granted dominance may have so distorted the historic meanings of Christian community as to render those meanings nearly impotent in their ability to address the deepest longings that the communal metaphor embodies.

In North American churches, it is a common-sense assumption that the church is located in a central place and that the pastor as symbolic leader of the community of believers is best located in the center of the community as the focal figure around which the community gathers. In an odd way this assumption has perhaps become more commonly taken for granted across the board in the Protestant churches with their varying traditions of the "priesthood of all believers" than in the Roman Catholic communion in America, where in recent years there has developed a strong lay movement, overtly public and covertly private, that presses against the centrality and authority of ecclesiastical leadership.

In its most exaggerated form, the centrist notion of the role of the pastor has become for many churches what in political circles would be called a "cult of personality." The congregation becomes "Pastor So-and-So's Church." Everything that goes on in the community of believers revolves around the pastor and is seen or evaluated in relation to the pastor's beliefs, desires, and proscriptions. In less personally focused and obtrusive fashion, many mainline Protestant congregations have come to take for granted what in theological academic circles is called the "clerical paradigm" as the way in which a viable Christian community can best sustain itself.

I would suggest that it is both revealing and potentially useful to schematize this clergy-centered community of faith in the following way (see Figure 1 on next page):

We see that the metaphorical and experiential placing of the pastoral leader in the center of the religious community tends almost inexorably to create a situation in which persons within that community must locate themselves at either greater or lesser distance within the orbit of pastoral leadership. An inner circle of persons who identify themselves with the leader is created. That identification may be charged with varying degrees of emotional commitment, of conferral of authority in matters of belief and practice upon the pastor, and of involvement in the decision making and organizational life of the community. Parenthetically, it may be said that many pastors when they think of "my people," think primarily of this inner circle. Furthermore, they may consider that one of their primary functions as pastoral leader is to draw as many people as possible into this inner circle. This includes attracting as many people as possible into involvement in as many of the programmatic activities of the congregation as possible. Words often used to speak of these efforts to draw persons toward the center are metaphors such as loyalty, faithfulness, and commitment.

Just outside the inner circle may be found those I have designated in the schematic as the outer circle. These are persons who for varying reasons have located themselves at a slightly greater distance from the focal core of the community and from the pastor. They may be seen regularly, or only occasionally, in Sunday morning worship. They may even be participants in selected programs and activities such as a church school class or a singles group. But their involvement with the pastor and with the inner circle is less visibly intense and encompassing. It is as if these persons have set limits on the centripetal attracting power of the core of the religious community symbolized by the pastor as central figure. For some in this outer circle it seems that there is another, perhaps more private and personal center to their religious life—a life to which the church community may in certain ways contribute. But that contribution

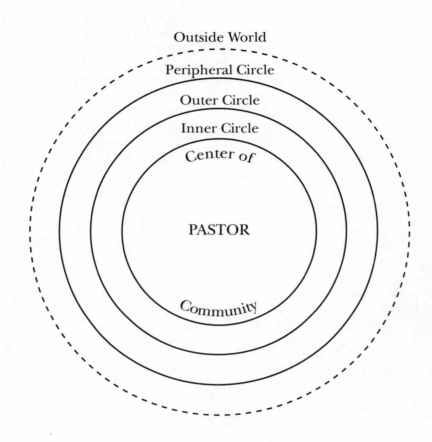

Figure 1

THE PASTOR-CENTERED COMMUNITY

is only partial and less demarcated by the church community for these persons than for those in the inner circle.

In the schema of Figure 1, the persons who psychologically and organizationally are at the greatest distance from the pastoral center of the community, while yet being related to it in sometimes significant ways, are those on the periphery. Seen only occasionally in the sanctuary of worship in the church, often perceived by those closer to the center as only marginally involved or inactive, these persons appear to turn toward the center and its central pastoral figure only when a felt need arises. Those times will most often include times of acute crisis such as serious illness or death, and perhaps the historic high holidays of the religious community such as Christmas or Easter. They may also, however, include less publicly visible occasions when privately motivated desire or felt relational conflict may prompt the person to touch base with the symbolic center of religious life and commitment. Most often seen by persons nearer the center of the community as nominal church members and therefore somehow less religious, they are considered part of what is often called the constituency of the church community. However, they appear to keep their emotional and physical distance.

Just beyond the quite permeable and only faintly demarcated boundary that contains the peripheral constituents of the church community in this schematization lies the outside world—the world outside the church with its own secular organizations, activities, and set of priorities for human involvement. Outside the boundaries of the religious community, that world is often thought of as alien and unaffected by the values, traditions, beliefs, and normative commitments to be found at the center of the life of the religious community. It is the outside world. Within that secular world, the church community may exercise its corporate mission, but the secular world in which most people, including Christians, must live and do the necessary work of the world is a world governed by norms, boundaries, authorities, and corporate structures quite unlike those of the church, which is alone designated the religious community.

UNINTENDED MEANING CONSEQUENCES OF THE CENTRIPETAL MODEL OF CHURCH

It would be my contention that the commonly accepted and virtually universally practiced model of the church schematized in Figure 1 is dominant in American society. It operates as an unexamined or seldom questioned common-sense understanding of the meaning and structure of a religious community. This understanding has brought about a number of consequent shifts in meaning that have had debilitating effects on the impact of the church at both personal and social levels. Its common-sense acceptance has likewise had profound effects on the common-sense understanding of the work of ministry in relation both to the religious community and to the so-called secular society. Within the purpose of this chapter, I shall here list only a few of those ramifications.

1. In the consciousness of ordinary persons in the society, understanding of the presence and activity of God as that presence and activity relates to human activity has been pressed into the confinement of the religious community and its places of worship and prayer.

The secular world has become increasingly seen as a world without God. The place where God's name is to be spoken is the place at the center of the religious community. In the secular world of business and industry, school and civic affairs, and art and leisure, another language is spoken—a language either devoid of religious meanings or in which those meanings are obscured by language that avoids reference to religious commitment. For many, even those who may belong to the inner or outer circles of the religious community as Figure 1 schematizes it, the use of God language in the affairs of everyday secular life has become embarrassing, even felt as somehow inappropriate. In any case, direct talk and reflection concerning the involvement of God in human affairs is squeezed out of the discourse of the secular marketplace and into the confines of the identified religious community. Both religion and religious community have become privatized and to that extent the church is seen no longer as a public community exercising active influence on public affairs.

2. Set in the meaning structure of Figure 1, the church as a magnetic community is experienced by many as one institutional center of attraction and activity in open competition with other centers, each of which competes for the loyalty and participation of persons.

This open marketplace of institutional loyalties and competing claims is accompanied by a common-sense understanding that each person can and should drive his or her own bargain for an individually determined implicit or explicit contract that parcels out one's involvement among various magnetic centers of human activity. Since each center is assumed to invite, even demand, a more or less total level of involvement, the burden of negotiating a balance among the pulls and tugs of competing loyalties rests on the shoulders of the individual—certainly a new and, religiously speaking, strange definition of "working out one's own salvation with fear and trembling."

3. Within this meaning structure, the chief, if not the only, way to be truly religious in one's orientation to life is to move closer to the inner circle of the identified religious community.

That means, at the very least, greater commitment of time and energy, and greater identification with the perceived center of religious loyalty embodied in the pastor as symbolic holder of the inside end of the tie that binds the individual to the central locus of the religious community. Metaphorically speaking, it is assumed that one of the pastor's primary roles in the community is to tug as strongly as possible on that tie in order to draw the individual closer to the church community and away from other centers of loyalty. "Thou shalt have no other gods before me" is transposed into "Thou shalt have no other loyalty before loyalty to the church."

Although this penchant for fixating the locus of religious loyalty to a particular institution and its physical location as we see it in contemporary American culture has a unique cast because of the way in which Western society has historically constructed its institutional life, the human tendency in that regard is by no means new. The question as to where to locate the center of religious commitment was one that troubled the people of the Bible from the earliest times of the patriarchs. Imagistically speaking, we can see the early practices of the Israelites in preserving the ark, a relic from a sacred historic location at Gilgal, as symbolically holding together their desire both to locate the center of the community and to be able to carry that symbolic locus of Yahweh's covenanting presence with them. The ark thus became both a location for their cultic faith and a portable center on their nomadic travels.[1] Later, when King David moved to establish the center of Israelite religion in Jerusalem, he had the ark moved to Jerusalem, thus preserving the traditional image "that Yahweh, who delivered his people from the land of Egypt, and accompanied them in their wanderings and battles leading to the occupation of their new land, was still at the center of David's Jerusalem cult."[2] Thus began the practice of a periodic pilgrimage to the now more or less permanently located center.

It must be acknowledged that cogent and persuasive arguments can be made on both historical and sociological grounds for the necessity of the church functioning as a discrete and separate institutional locus within a complex modern society. Without such an institutional structure, the world of religious faith and practice might well not survive in viable, identifiable ways. Nevertheless, it also can be argued that the acceptance of that necessity on the part of the religious community has served to reinforce the tendency *in the common-sense mind of the people* to locate their religious activities and sensibilities exclusively in the religious institution and its affairs, thus leaving open the possibility of a sterilization of so-called secular institutions and their activities of religious meaning. It likewise leaves open the possibility that a considerable number of people for whom the penchant for organizational, institutional activity, such as goes on near the center of the life of most churches, is minimal may, metaphorically speaking, be left on their own carrying what relics are left of their sacred "ark" around with them in an alien, secular world, but doing so without the benefit of an identifiable religious community.

The common-sense location of the meanings of religion in the centers of activity in the churches is all too often duplicated in the common-sense minds of the clergy. Not only do many pastors identify the religious people of the community with those who are centripetally drawn toward the center of activity of the churches (all too often even more specifically the center of their own local church), but also they tend to experience themselves as on alien ground when they are in a so-called secular context or not attending closely to the organizational and programmatic life of the institutional church. To the extent that this is the case, the division of institutions into sacred and secular in the common-sense minds of the people is reinforced. In that situation, any notion of a "community of God's people"—in the holistic sense involving all of life's activities and institutions—tends to become fragmented, or at best, badly obscured.

Reflecting about this phenomenon, one is reminded of the subtle but definite and meaning-altering shifts that have taken place in recent times in the meaning of the terms *parish* and *parishioner*. In its original English usage, the word *parish* referred to a British church district with its own church. It included all of the activities that took place in that geographical location and all of the people who lived there who were considered to be under the care of the church and its ministry, whether or not they were near the center of its organizational life. The term had and continues to have that same meaning in Roman Catholic usage. Seen within that meaning context, the parish metaphor bridged the sharp division between sacred and secular. In more recent usage, particularly in America, however, the common-sense usage of the term *parish*, particularly among mainline Protestant clergy and laity, has come to be identified only with those who specifically hold membership in a particular local congregation and with the activities that go on in that congregation. Again, the division of the community of institutions and persons into sacred and secular, on the one hand, and member and non-member of the religious community, on the other hand, has been reinforced, and the fragmentation of the larger community of persons and institutions quietly fostered.

4. One of the unanticipated results of the common-sense appropriation of the centripetal model of religious community in American religious life—a result often verbally lamented by mainline liberal clergy and sometimes quite openly exploited by conservative and fundamentalist evangelicals—is that it has served to foster the formation of religious communities of people who value their sameness with one another rather than their diversity.

That sameness has then tended to include sameness in beliefs, in race and class, in social attitudes, in economic presuppositions, and the like. The religious community as a fellowship of kindred minds has thus tended to become insular from interaction with the pluralism of the world in ways that are both stultifying and fundamentally disloyal to biblical metaphorical images of the church as embodying all of the people of God. Instead of the church being experienced as a servant people whose mission is to be found out in the world in service to all, the peoples of the world are quietly, if unintentionally, divided into those who are like us and those who are strangers.

It is edifying to note that into this common-sense, taken-for-granted understanding of the fellowship of kindred minds notion of religious community has been thrust the interruptive presence of the homeless in virtually all American communities in recent years. So great and so visible has been their need that they simply cannot be overlooked. One by one, the churches located in the inner city and then even many of the most insulated suburban congregations have opened their physical doors to offer shelter to these often unattractive, even undesirably strange, people. One by one, those who have become involved in service to these who are literally without a home have been confronted with their kinship with strangers with whom they would ordinarily avoid association. They have made contact with persons with the same hopes and fears as their own who do not possess the same protections against the cold and indifference of the world that they possess. For more than one member of an otherwise insulated religious community, this confrontation with the homeless poor has been, in the phrase of H. Richard Niebuhr, a confrontation with the actions of God hidden in the actions of others upon them.

It is sadly edifying to note also, that the response of religious communities to the human degradation of poverty and homelessness has not always been to hear the voice of God calling them out of their isolation from the pain of the world. More than one congregation has taken the presence of such people and their problems as a signal that it is time to relocate their religious ark to the safer, more comfortable environs of the suburbs. Frightened by the presence of the poor, so often accompanied by the presence of petty crime and potential violence, these communities—like the Smallberg Church of the last chapter—have elected to create a safer, less troubled sanctuary.

THE DESIRE AND RISKS OF COMMUNITY: THE MICROCOSM OF A CLINICAL EXAMPLE

We shall return later to further reflections on the problem of metaphorical meanings of community in the situation of the contemporary church and the role of pastoral practice in fostering a reclamation of the root biblical meanings of community. At this point, however, it may be useful to dislocate ourselves from the familiarity of the pastoral role as keeper of the centripetal center of the religious community to see what appears when the pastor is thrust into an unfamiliarly strange place. To achieve that dislocation, I shall turn our attention to a situation that took place in a clinical pastoral education program sponsored by a cluster of medical facilities located in and around a large metropolitan city. As the case study unfolds, we will pause from time to time to reflect on what is occurring in relation to the task of this chapter concerning the search for community.

The occasion that brought this situation to my attention was a gathering of all of the pastors and seminarians, along with their clinical supervisors, who were participating in the several institutions and clinical pastoral education programs in the cluster. I was present in the role of consultant and commentator. The announced theme for the morning-long conference was the theme of development of community in the midst of diversity.

As is very often the case in clinical pastoral education programs, the morning began with the presentation of a case study by one of the students. She and her immediate peer group gathered in the center of a larger circle composed of the students and supervisors of the other programs. As consultant-observer, I located myself as a member of that larger circle. The student then presented the following description of a ministry situation in which she had recently been involved:

Barely thirty minutes after I began the On-Call duty the beeper went on. It was calling me to go answer a death call on Unit 6-1. I sought out

126

the person (fellow student) assigned to that unit, but my peer was not in the hospital. I decided that I needed to answer the call personally.

The call was to be with the lover of a homosexual, white male in his late twenties who had died of AIDS. There were no other relatives nor family there. I thought it would be a short visit, as in other cases, but I was in for a big surprise. This had been an unexpected death, so the lover was thoroughly distraught with grief and guilt, and an AIDS victim himself.

When I arrived at the floor I went directly to the patient's room, but the deceased patient was alone. Then I went to the quiet room; nobody was there either. I inquired at the nurses station. They helped me look, but we couldn't find the man anywhere. Suddenly, they saw him walking out of the men's restroom, and they pointed him out to me and the administrative nurse introduced us. What follows is a brief verbatim of our encounter:

N. J., this is the chaplain.
E. Hi, J. I'm Edith L., one of the ministers in the hospital.
    I understand that you have had a great loss.
J. Hi. Will you talk to me?

Hearing this initial greeting of the minister by the grieving homosexual lover, we are struck immediately by the tentative expression of his longing for community. "Will you talk to me?" It is the cry of the outcast who both desires someone, even a stranger, to share his time of grief and expects to be rebuffed. We can guess that for him the representative of the church embodies both the meaning of a potential community of care and of exclusion. As one who wears the labels assigned to the homosexual and the victim of AIDS, he expects the representative of the inner circle of religious life to exclude him from the circle of care. Nevertheless, his need is great. So he makes the request. "Will you talk to me?"

The conversation continues. In the verbatim report of it, however, Edith, the chaplain, must first acknowledge her own tentativeness about forming community with this stranger.

I noticed that his face was swollen due to the crying. I placed a chair almost directly in front of him, very close. I remembered that the nurse had told me over the phone that he had AIDS and she thought I should know. So as I placed the chair in front of him I remembered that he was an AIDS victim and that I should take every precaution necessary. I did not, however, change the position of the chair, because I felt that he needed someone to be close. The thought occurred to me that if he had been a woman, I would probably have simply sat beside him on the sofa in the room.

J.   Is he dead; is he really dead? (With great sobs and tears)

E.   Yes, he is really dead. (Embracing him)

J.   I should have been with him more time. But I was afraid. I could not hold him as he wanted. I should of known. He told me he felt like on a roller-coaster and that he wanted to get off.

E.   He did get off.

J.   Yes he did. And he died alone. I did not want him to die alone. I missed him by two minutes. I didn't know that he was in the hospital. I came as soon as I knew, and I missed him by two minutes. (Now he began to cry and speak very loudly in his cry) I don't want to die alone! I don't want to die alone!

Now he was crying so hard I couldn't resist embracing him, trying to hold him in order to give him some comfort. He was not only crying for the loss, but for his own death he was foreseeing would be as lonely as his lover's death. As he cried, tears fell on my arms and some mucus too when he moved. I felt like letting him go to dry myself up, but feared for his well-being. I could smell the smell of a sick body. As I write this I can still smell it.

We see that both Edith and J. have become acutely aware of the absence of community in the situation in which they find themselves. J. is overcome with his feelings of remorse over not being with his friend at the time of his death. He is also flooded with the loneliness of his own situation. Sensitive as she is to the overpowering loneliness she has been drawn into, Edith, the minister, reaches out to offer J. community with her. But she is also acutely aware of the risks involved. His bodily fluids—the bodily fluids of an AIDS victim—are mingling with her own tears on her own body! How much risk can she afford to take to make community with this stranger? (Parenthetically, it needs to be said that Edith's fears for her own safety may not be realistic. Medical authorities are themselves not completely clear about this. On the one hand, medical opinion seems to be that the risks of infection by the AIDS virus through this kind of bodily contact are somewhat remote. On the other hand, there are recorded incidents of infection of medical personnel despite the use of ordinary precautions. The supervising nurse's warning to Edith prior to her introduction to J. is indicative of the uncertainty of risk in the situation.)

E.   You are not alone now; you are not alone. (As I continued to hold him.) Remember your parents and your friends. You are not alone.

He straightened up and I sought a box of Kleenex and dried up my own tears along with his tears and mucus from my arm. He was looking at me straight in the eyes.

E.   I want to tell you something I hope you can hear. We all die alone. We do not take anyone with us when we die; we do it alone, just as when we are born we are born alone. We all have the same fear of dying alone. But you do not have to die being completely alone because you have your parents and your friends. How is your relationship with your parents and your friends?

J.   Oh, yes, all is fine with us. My parents love me and my friends do love me, too. I have to have more friends though. You know I want to live; I do not want to die. I want to live. I was told by everyone that this would kill me. So I had to stay away from him. My therapist told me and my mom told me. I had been away for about a year until I was told he was sick, too. He had kicked me out. But I didn't know that he was sick, too. I didn't give it to him. I feel so guilty.

Edith is pressed to inquire about the availability of a community of caring others that can support J. in his situation of bereavement and loss. Recognizing that the community of care she is offering is itself only symbolic and temporary, she desires to point J. toward whatever sustaining community may be available to him. Her inquiry thus represents an important decision involving a choice regarding the purpose of pastoral care ministry. It is significant that neither does she rely simply on the communal relationship she is offering J. at the moment, nor does she inquire concerning J.'s relationship to an identified religious community. Her purpose seems not to be that of drawing J. closer to the inner circle of such a community, but rather to remind him of the significance of whatever community he can claim.

At this point Edith and J. moved from the quiet room to the room where the dead body of J.'s friend still lay. Edith, in reporting this portion of the incident to the student group, indicated that she was during this time still quite confused in her feelings between her desire to be in communion with this distraught man and her fear of contamination. She spoke of feeling strangely guilty, but also compassionate.

E.   What do you feel so guilty about?

J.   I don't know. I don't know. Oh God, Oh God, Oh God. (He sobbed more and more. I thought to myself: Oh my God, I'm going to lose this fellow. I might need extra help with him. He seems to be getting worse. I thought of it but decided not to offer a spoken prayer for him at that moment.)

E.   You two really had an intense relationship going on. I'm glad for
     you that you can cry this way because it helps to get it off your
     chest. I'm also glad that you want to live. I like that.
J.   Yes, I want to live. I want to . . . (Pause)
E.   You want to . . .
J.   I want to live. I want to be fulfilled.
E.   What would it take for you to be fulfilled?
J.   (After a thoughtful silence) I want to achieve . . . (Again silence)
E.   What do you want to achieve?
J.   I want to help people and I want to be respected for what I do?
     (J.'s statement ends in the tone of a question. He then fell silent
     again, but after a time began to nod his head as if to affirm what
     he had said.) But I want to be fulfilled. (Another silence.)
E.   Would you tell me of your relationship with him. How was it to
     love him? (J. then talked quietly and warmly of his relationship
     with his dead friend.)
E.   Would you be able to say that you were fulfilled in this
     relationship?
J.   Yes, very much so. But now I am alone.
E.   Yes, you have had a great loss.

Just what J. means by his wish to be fulfilled never becomes clear in the
conversation as it is reported. On reflection, we can perhaps speculate
that hidden in that wish for fulfillment is J.'s inchoate desire for a
broader, richer experience of community with his fellow human beings.
It hints vaguely at a desire for more significance. This is particularly
apparent from his expressed wish to "help people and be respected for
what I do." The flaw in his limited experience with others cramped
perhaps by his involvement in homosexuality and the AIDS syndrome is
tentatively exposed. We might wish that Edith had chosen to explore with
J. what is seeking expression in these hints at unfulfillment. She, however,
chooses to invite instead a fuller expression of J.'s relationship with his
dead friend.
Edith's report of the conversation continues:

By this time a friend of J.'s arrived. As he walked in J. began to cry
again loudly.
J.   He's dead! He's dead! I missed him by only two minutes.
(J.'s friend hugged him tightly and closely as a mother would do to a
child as J. continued to cry with great sobs. The sight of this was very
tender and warm to watch. I watched in silence, not even saying
anything when the friend would make a comment with which I would

agree. I was deeply touched by the expression of love between these two males who were being so very feminine in their expression of love and support to each other in their loss. As I write this, I feel gratitude for having witnessed such expressions of love and care.

The friend assured J. that he would not be alone and that he would come through alright. They then began to make plans for the funeral. Soon after, they began to prepare to leave.)

E.   May the Lord be with you and strengthen and comfort you and may the Holy Spirit come to give you peace.

Edith then ends her report of her ministry in this situation with a description of her thoughts and actions immediately after it was over.

I said my farewells; they said their thank yous and I left. I searched for the bathroom and washed my arms and hands. I looked for the administrative nurse to let her know that I was leaving. She told me they had expressed their thanks to her for my being there with them. I thanked her and was on my way. I didn't want to touch anyone. I walked into the office and as soon as possible went to the apartment to wash my hands and face again. I feared for my health and the health of others and I prayed for continued health and the hope of not having tempted God with the risk I took at being with this young man. Perhaps I will never forget his eyes of gratitude and his smile for me when I left him, but I probably will also never forget the fear over my health being in jeopardy, either.

In her oral presentation to her peer group, Edith reflected further at great length about the levels of confrontation she experienced in this unexpected ministry opportunity. She spoke of being deeply impressed with the tenderness and open expression of care she observed between the two homosexual men and said that she was struck with the realization that "I have not seen that quality of expression in heterosexual relationships at the moment of grief among husband and wife, friends, nor relatives, parents and siblings." She also was confronted with her deep and previously unclaimed fear of AIDS and abhorrence of homosexuality. It had even stirred in her an awareness of her fears about her teenage son's struggle with gender-identity issues. Furthermore, she had been confronted sharply with the risks involved in being the ordained representative of the Christian community of care with strangers afflicted with a deadly disease. Most particularly in that regard, she had been made aware of the conflicts she experienced between what she found herself doing in this situation and the commonly accepted attitudes of her denomination toward homosexuality and AIDS.

In summary, Edith reported that the experience of ministry with the persons with AIDS had been for her an experience of profound dislocation that had forced her to reexamine many of the common sense notions she had about community and communion among persons. The deep needs of all human beings for a community of care had been exposed, along with the subtle and taken-for-granted ways in which boundaries are established that separate people from one another and protect communities from the stranger in their midst.

The extended discussion that ensued in, first, Edith's immediate peer learning group and later in the larger circle, probed—at first hesitantly and then more passionately and urgently—into some of the wider ramifications of Edith's critical incident of ministry for an understanding of issues related to the human need and desire for community. The tendency of all human communities to set boundaries that limit risks and demarcate the differences between inside and outside was explored, along with the ways in which inside tends to become privatized and outside tends to become imaged as alien. To move toward a community of the whole people of God seems to depend on finding ways to break through the human need for privacy, yet that is in tension with the human need for safety, something separate and autonomously self-contained.

The question was explored as to what it is, finally, that makes a community safe. The recognition seems necessary that, theologically speaking, the safety of any community is finally not dependent upon human construction of boundaries and centripetal structures of organization, but on trust in the creative activity of God in the creation of an ultimate community of all things. Our human efforts to create centers of community safe from the risks of relationship to a larger ecology that transcends those centers can become idolatrous. Intrusions such as Edith had experienced serve to remind us of that theological reality and break open our communities of sameness and safety.

IMAGINING THE POSSIBILITY OF A CENTRIFUGAL MODEL OF CHRISTIAN COMMUNITY

I have spoken of the report of Pastor Edith L.'s experience of ministry with the grieving homosexual AIDS victim and its discussion in the Clinical Pastoral Education conference as a dislocation from the accustomed locus of Christian community within the centripetal imagery of the church. Pastor L. found herself in an alien place in pastoral dialogue with one whom she experienced as well outside the circular boundaries of her religious community. Her pastoral instinct was to seek to find community with this stranger and to remind and inquire concerning whatever community of care existed in his life.

I propose that we imaginatively reflect on this incident of ministry outside the accustomed boundaries of the church community as an extended metaphor that may open up consideration of a model of Christian community counter to the enclosed, centripetal model discussed earlier.[3] In doing so, my intention is not totally to negate the value or the institutional necessity of the centripetal model. Rather, my desire is to place it in tension with another model suggested by the extended metaphor in search of a corrective for the common-sense appropriation of the centripetal model by both laity and clergy.

Simply reflecting on the two terms *dislocation* and *centrifugal* begins to open up some potentially transformative imagery. Both terms conjure up images of dispersal of the Christian community outside its own boundaries into the larger world of human affairs. Centrifugal implies a move away from a center.[4] To embrace a centrifugal image of the Christian community will thus necessitate the valuing of movement of Christians out into the world away from the central locus of their community. The centrifugal force of such a model will, therefore, counter the tug of commitment of persons toward the inner circle with a thrust into the secular world outside the orbit of the central Christian locus. Dislocation into the world will be the *modus operandi* of such a community, rather than location in a center of worship and community apart from or separated from the secular world. Involvement in the affairs of the world, rather than privacy of commitment away from the world, will be the expectation and invitation of such a community. Members of such communities will not only expect to be dislocated, but will seek such dislocations in order that the catalyst of Christian communal meanings may do its work in the many and varied locations to be found in the world.

BIBLICAL WISDOM CONCERNING THE CENTRIFUGAL MODEL

Taking our cue from the work done in chapter 2 regarding the transformation of common sense by way of reappropriation of the deepest metaphorical wisdom of a tradition, we are prompted to turn to reflection on certain of the primal biblical narratives of community for normative guidance in evaluating the appropriateness of a centrifugal model for Christian community. Do the biblical narratives of community provide trustworthy normative guidance for such a model?

In writing about the early beginnings of the Israelite community as a self-identified people of God, Paul Hanson in his book, *The People Called*, has this to say:

> From those called to be God's people a response was required that was patterned after God's holiness. Holiness was the quality that characterized the God Yahweh, and the command for communal holiness is to be understood in relation to Israel's deeply felt dependence on God's abiding presence. The people could be confident of God's presence with them only if their life together was a reflection of God's nature and of God's concern for justice. In Israel's earliest attempts to express this notion of community, the dominant pattern was that of *imitatio dei:* to assure Yahweh's continued presence with the people meant acting toward other humans even as Yahweh had first acted toward them.[5]

A primary implication of this understanding of the Israelite community as called to imitate the holiness of God comes from the early biblical understanding that Yahweh does not choose to stay apart from the affairs of the world, but chooses rather to be actively engaged in the world of human affairs seeking to fulfill Yahweh's own purposes. The God of Israel is an active, passionate God concerned for both the preservation of the community of God's people and the welfare of all. Said plainly and straightforwardly, the God Yahweh does not choose to stay aloof from the affairs of the world. Yahweh moves out from Yahweh's self in acts of compassion and justice. So also should Yahweh's people.

Hanson traces carefully the growth and development of this central idea of Israel's notion of community. In the narrative concerning Second Isaiah, he finds a culmination and confirmation of this primal understanding in the texts concerning Israel as a servant people.

> I am the Lord, I have called you in righteousness,
>   I have taken you by the hand and kept you;
> I have given you as a covenant to the people,
>   a light to the nations,
>   to open the eyes that are blind,
> to bring out the prisoners from the dungeon,
>   from the prison those who sit in darkness.
> (Isa. 42:6-7)

Concerning this text, Hanson says:

It is difficult to grasp the magnitude of the change in Israel's vocation implied in the transition from being "my servant to raise up the tribes of Jacob and restore the preserved of Israel" to becoming "a light to the nations, that my salvation may reach to the end of the earth." (Isaiah 49:6) Such a move was made possible only as the historical consequence of a vastly enlarged vision of Yahweh's majesty.[6]

Imaginative reflection on Hanson's interpretation of these biblical texts, when placed in the context of our consideration of centripetal versus centrifugal models of Christian community, places before us the possible analogy between the self absorption of the centripetal model and the earliest concerns of the people of Israel for their own identification with God and God's purposes. The call of the texts of Second Isaiah strike us as potentially and powerfully analogous to the call of the centrifugal model to dislocate the people called Christian from their own tribal preoccupations into a larger, centrifugal ministry in the world.

THE CENTRIFUGAL MODEL RECONSIDERED

With those images from the prophet Isaiah before us, we now return to our reflections on the dislocation of the Christian pastor, Edith L., armed with what seems to be deeper, richer imagistic wisdom. Edith may have found herself in a strange, alienated, dislocated place in her effort to minister to the grieving homosexual man with AIDS. But, if the wisdom of Isaiah provides normative criteria, she was in the right place—a place far from the central locus of the Christian community she represented, but a place where God's concern for justice and love for all God's people prompted her to be. Like most dislocated places out in the world away from the sanctuaried center of Christian community, it was a place of risk and ambiguity. It was a place among strangers. But, it was undoubtedly the place where the imitators of God's concern for those in need are called to be. Furthermore, Edith's instinct to act to nourish and encourage the viability of what community she found there, rather than simply following the centripetal instinct to tug J. closer to the center of the visible, institutional Christian community, takes on a more genuine, biblically based authenticity. It authentically expresses an imitation of God's concern for the community of all people, and not simply or exclusively the self-identified members of those circles close to the center of worship. Its primary interest is centrifugal; it seeks to spin off the communion at the heart of Christian experience into places out in the world wherever the need for communion is to be found.

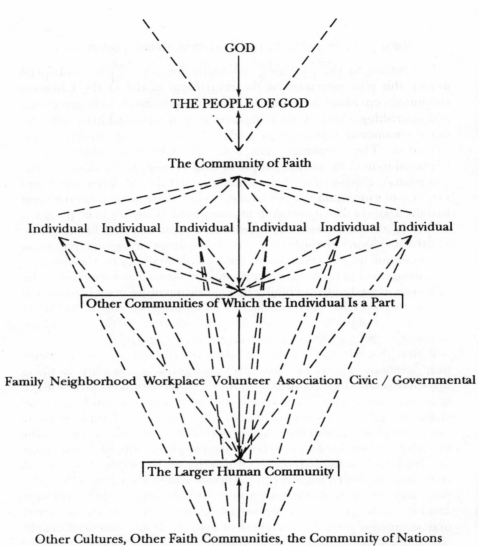

GOD

THE PEOPLE OF GOD

The Community of Faith

Individual   Individual   Individual   Individual   Individual   Individual

Other Communities of Which the Individual Is a Part

Family Neighborhood Workplace Volunteer Association Civic / Governmental

The Larger Human Community

Other Cultures, Other Faith Communities, the Community of Nations

The Physical / Environmental World

Figure 2

THE GOD/PEOPLE OF GOD-CENTERED IMAGE OF COMMUNITY

In contrast to the confining, enclosing imagery of the centripetal model, this schematization of the centrifugal model of the Christian community envisions that community as primarily involved in preserving and nourishing a body of meanings and style of relationship by which all other communal relationships are to be understood, fostered, and evaluated. The meanings that hold the Christian community in relationship to God and the people of God as they are inculcated in the Christian community are thus to be disbursed into all other levels and varieties of community relationships, rather than to be treasured and harbored within the Christian community itself. They are to be placed in service to all other levels of communal relationships and brought into creative dialogue with the bodies of meaning that arise within other forms of communal life. The Christian community thus finds its vocation and self realization not by preoccupying itself with its own activities and circles of involvement, but by becoming dialogically involved in and committed to the enhancement of other loci of communal life. In the words of Second Isaiah, the Christian community fulfills itself as it becomes "a light to the nations."

Within this schematic image of Christian community, involvements with locations where the human longing for community is being thwarted, such as that in which the pastor, Edith L., found herself, will not be seen in the image of dislocation and strangeness so much as in the image of right and proper location, the placement of representative Christians in service to those whose experience of community cries out for the leaven of Christian meanings and meaningful action. In the language developed in earlier chapters of this book, the realization of the centrifugal model of Christian community involves bringing to bear the deep and rich metaphorical wisdom of the Christian tradition in every arena of worldly activity where issues of community are at stake. Rather than competing with other centers of activity for the time and energy commitments of persons—attempting to pull persons away from other centers of activity and into the activity of the centripetal community of the church—the fulfillment of the church's activity will be realized as those other centers of activity are infused with the results of dialogue with the God-given wisdom of the Christian community's tradition.

THE LOCATION OF THE PASTOR IN THE CENTRIFUGAL MODEL

The schema of Figure 2 implies a significant tension between its implied understanding of the role and location of the ordained pastor of the Christian community and that of the schema of Figure 1. In the centripetal model, the pastor is symbolically and functionally located in the center of the inner circle of the community. That location is, to be sure, not without both biblical and longstanding historical justification and rationale. As the ordained priest of the community, the pastor is the leader of worship and sacrament, the central meaning making and devotional activity of the Christian community. The pastor is also the chief interpreter of the historic texts and memories of the community in the instructive and educational act of the presentation of the preached word. All those acts of ministry belong in the center of the community's life. On the occasion of the gathering of the community, that central place of leadership is the proper location for the pastor.

The centrifugal model schematized in Figure 2, however, suggests a quite different location for the pastor in the work of ministry both in relation to the Christian community itself and in the larger community of God's people wherever they may be found at the many levels of communal life that schema outlines. Within that schema the pastor, rather than constantly maintaining his or her grasp on the inner end of the tie that binds the individual Christian to the inner circle of the church, is envisioned as moving from place to place—often in odd locations where there is need for nurturance and healing of the disruptions and injuries of community wherever they may be. The ministry of Edith L. in the case study presented to the clinical pastoral education conference appears as a useful and informative metaphorical lens through which the question of location of the pastor in the ordinary, non-ceremonial work of ministry may be envisioned. It is a locating of the pastor in the midst of a great variety of situations and contexts where problems of community are being encountered.

LEVELS OF INVOLVEMENT IN COMMUNITY
IN THE CENTRIFUGAL MODEL

The schema of Figure 2 is only suggestive of the broad sweep of levels of involvement in the human problem of community with which the core meanings of community preserved and celebrated by Christians are to be brought into dialogue centrifugally. While it is beyond the scope of this book to engage in a detailed analysis of the implications of a centrifugal model of Christian community at all of the widening levels the schema of Figure 2 proposes, the following listing of levels close at hand, and thus immediately available for the work of both pastoral and lay ministry, is suggestive of the possibilities of transformation of common-sense notions of the communal ministry of the church in the larger world.

1. The closest level to the individual is undoubtedly the level of family life.

Here a whole range of issues, problems, dilemmas, and common-sense understandings await the leaven of Christian discernment and action. At one end of the spectrum are issues of life within the traditionally predominant nuclear family made up of father, mother, and one or more children. How is such a family to structure itself, its governance, its intimate affectional ties, and its involvements in the world so that it functions as an authentic community of Christian nurture? Are the communal metaphors that have traditionally shaped the nuclear family structure, such as those of paternalism and parental authority, any longer viable, or must they be replaced with more egalitarian, democratic, and developmental metaphorical images? Are there common-sense appropriations of biblical textual sources concerning family governance and decision making that need to be reexamined in open, inquiring conversation among members of nuclear families?

At the other end of the spectrum lies a host of problems and dilemmas relative to the increasing number of persons who live in single parent homes, alone, or are without family and/or homeless. The alienation and high mobility of much of contemporary life create living situations for countless persons that seem not to support even rudimentary remnants of familial community. The Christian community seen in the image of servanthood and nurturer of community is called out of its insular self-preoccupation into interaction and self-sacrificing engagement with all the problematic nooks and crannies of family living, including such contemporary front page issues as extra-familial child and infant care, family violence and child abuse, divorce and the fractured or reconstituted family, aging families, and family members who are no longer able to care for themselves, and the like.

2. The neighborhood controversy through which we encountered the narrative structure of common sense in chapter 2 revealed only a limited few of the many facets of the problem of community in the neighborhoods of modern American cities.

Here are to be found not only the constricting tendencies of communities to become private enclaves insulated from the problems of the city found in the suburban sprawls that take up the desirable outlying space of most metropolitan communities, but also the chaos and social disorganization caused by poverty and overcrowding in much of the deteriorating core of city life. Here also lie the issues and ethical dilemmas hidden in the so-called gentrification of an increasing number of urban neighborhoods. As these neighborhoods gentify, their former residents are crowded ever closer into less and less desirable housing at the risk of destruction of any sense of community among the people whatsoever. Through such creative projects as Habitat for Humanity, Christians are being called out of their centripetal centers of activity into engagement with the needs of their poorer brothers and sisters for a place to call home in which they can take prideful ownership.

3. Christian concern for community among God's people must search diligently for ways to engage the increasingly regimented and bureaucratic modes of community to be found in the American workplace.

Here, as perhaps in no other location, the reign of secularization seems increasingly supreme. The gods of the bottom line of profitability, consumerism, and self-aggrandizing corporate purpose inform the rule of common sense. All other considerations of community and care for persons seem subservient to the fulfillment of company policy and corporate purpose. Loyalty to God and God's purposes must either be replaced by loyalty to the secular goals of the company, or submerged in private thoughts of workers and correlated with company loyalty as best one can manage for oneself. In common-sense practice, an often vague and unexamined mindset develops that so merges images of participation in the workaday world with images of Christian vocation as to see that activity as coincidental with devotion to the way God intended the human working world to be.

Hearing the problem of community stated in such harshly critical terms may sound unduly polemical. Surely there are to be found in many corporate work environments pockets of genuine, mutually supportive, and satisfying community where persons find realistic appreciation for their productivity and nurture of their needs to participate in a worthwhile community endeavor. Yet the stories of corporate greed and exploitation of persons, most notably persons working at lower levels of business and industry, continue to flow across the pages of the daily newspaper. Metaphors such as "the rat race," "it's a jungle out there," and "the salt mine" speak eloquently of the level of human awareness of a lack of nurturance in the communities of America's working life.

Across the years of my experience of listening to mostly middle class American workers who became unhappy enough to seek pastoral counseling, I have observed a common wishful fantasy, the wish to "go into business for myself." Examined, the fantasy most often contains the desire to create a place of work where one would not have to be exposed to demeaning conformities to the impersonal, heavy-handed corporate will of an employing corporation, but rather create a working community that cared for persons in their individuality.

One such counselee became able over a period of several years to realize that wish in a rather remarkable way. An exceptionally talented electronic expert who was also a recovering alcoholic when I first met him, he nurtured a dream throughout his struggle to recover to own his own company. Because of his recognized talent, he was able to interest a group of business friends to make an investment in the promise of that talent, which enabled him to assemble a small group of technical workers to produce products of his inventive genius. From the beginning, he labored at fulfilling his vision by insisting on a thoroughgoing communal approach to corporate decision making that stretched all the way from the board of directors to the workers on the small assembly line he put together.

An important symbolic development of the community this man engendered in the working environment of his company came about the first spring after the plant opened. There was a large vacant piece of land at the back of the company property. He proposed at a called meeting of all his workers that they undertake a community vegetable and flower garden on the vacant lot. Most of the workers were enthusiastic, seeing in the project not only an added opportunity to do something meaningful together, but also a chance to help their family grocery budgets. The question arose as to whether work on the garden was to be done on company time or whether they would have to do the work on their own time. It was agreed that both were possible, assuming they could organize themselves so that the assembly work of the plant would not be unduly interrupted. So it was done, much to the communal joy of the workers and, even more, to the joyful fulfillment of what was once only a wistful fantasy of an alienated and lonely alcoholic electronics engineer.

Up to the present, with few exceptions, the ministry of the Christian community in the working environment has consisted largely of one or the other of two types of facilitative services designed to be of help to individuals. One such ministry, commonly called an industrial chaplaincy, and ordinarily staffed by one or more ordained clergypersons, is most often designed to provide supportive pastoral services and counseling to workers who become victims of either the stresses of work or, more often, the problems of family and individual life made more difficult by the practices of the company in relation to their workers.

Individually focused, these ministries, while helpful, most often fall short of addressing the communal structures that affect the needs of persons in the workplace.

A second, often hidden and less openly church sponsored or recognized lay ministry of community in the working world is, of course, that of committed laypersons who as a natural expression of their Christian vocation exercise in either self-identified or unselfconscious ways their influence to affect corporate policies and personnel practices in fundamentally Christian directions. Within the centrifugal model of Christian community being developed here, the activities of these persons would be seen as aspects of the Christian community's life beyond and outside of its ordinarily identified common-sense location.

The schema of Figure 2 projects centrifugal involvement of the Christian community at ever-widening levels of corporate life both within and beyond the immediate orbit of day-to-day activity in the lives of its members. The detailing of the above list of three such levels should therefore be understood as only suggestive of the possibilities that await the Christian congregation that begins to turn its attention away from its centripetal preoccupations outward toward a servant vocation in the world. Rather than attempting here to present an exhaustive and detailed survey of those possibilities, however, the limits of purpose of this book require that our attention be turned toward a more substantive examination of the normative dimensions of the vocation of Christians in the contemporary socio-cultural situation. Taking this turn does not mean to turn away from the images of community considered in this chapter. Rather, the work of the next chapter will be to examine those metaphors that comprise the theme of vocation in such a way as to give further shape to the thematics of presence and community already before us.

CHAPTER SIX

NORMATIVE METAPHORS FOR PASTORAL WORK:

Vocation

The theme of the final chapter of this book is in reality a theme that underlies the entire book, namely, that of the vocation or calling of the Christian community in the world of contemporary American culture. As the book's title suggests, our task in the pilgrimage of this book has been to discern appropriate and compelling Christian images of life together in the world in which we find ourselves. Earlier chapters have developed the notion that the recovery of a Christian understanding of life together involves a reappropriation of the deep and primary imagistic and metaphorical wisdom of the tradition that shapes Christian understanding. For the work of ministry, it involves an effort to transform the common-sense wisdom of persons and communities whose self understanding has been shaped in multiform ways by the twists and turns of socio-cultural change over centuries since those primal images and metaphors first exercised their formative power.

In the work of the last two chapters I proposed that the recovery of a profound Christian sense of life together involves first a reexamination of the meaning of Christian presence in the world. Our understanding of Christian presence has become fragmented and is badly in need of a resensitization to the presence of God in the world. It is an abiding sensitivity to God's presence and conformity to the purposes of divine presence that, if recovered with discernment and vision, can transform the contemporary common-sense meanings of Christian presence in ways that recover the deepest wisdom of our tradition.

A recovery of Christian presence in the world requires, secondly, a reexamination and reappropriation of images of Christian community. I have suggested that the turn of American cultural life toward the privatization of religion has, when conjoined with the development of centripetal models in the organization of religious communities, tended to create self-enclosed Christian communities cut off from the larger world of human affairs. The fulfillment of the Christian calling requires that these centripetal models of Christian community be countered with what was in chapter 5 labeled centrifugal, more public models. Without losing touch with their centers of ritual, worship, and reflection, Christian communities need to recover a rich variety of dialogical contact with other centers of communal life in the contemporary world.

The work that remains to be done in this final chapter involves the more specific employment of the lens provided by the thematic of vocation itself as a normative metaphorical lever for breaking open the Christian meaning of life together in the pluralistic, fragmented American cultural situation. By envisioning the task to which American Christians are called through the angle of vision provided by the theme of vocation, my hope and expectation is that the transformative possibilities of both Christian presence and Christian community may be further clarified and enriched.

HISTORICAL PERMUTATIONS IN THE MEANING OF VOCATION

Drawing from a classic article by the Lutheran church historian Karl Holl, titled "The History of the Word Vocation," my colleague at Emory University, James W. Fowler, has briefly and helpfully set forth the ways in which the meaning of the term *vocation* has changed significantly through the long years of Christian history.[1] In the biblical tradition, the term has been closely linked with the word *calling*. It has traditionally, says Fowler,

> Referred to God's calling of particular persons or groups into a special relation with God. God's call to Abraham brought him into a covenant relation that eventually formed a partnership people. God's call to Moses led to the liberation of Israel from slavery and to the joining of a new covenant, under Torah, at Sinai. We remember Isaiah, Jeremiah, Amos, and those figures we call the lesser prophets, as persons with a calling. Nehemiah in exile, the Hebrew cupbearer to the Babylonian king, felt a calling to return to Jerusalem, the broken and corrupted capital, to lead in the rebuilding of its walls and the purification of its people. And in their own ways, Sarah, Judith, Naomi, Ruth, and even Rahab were called and in their faithfulness gave over their lives to furthering the purposes of God.[2]

In New Testament times, the notion of a particular people's calling from God became linked with the usage of the Greek term *ecclesia*, which "means literally a 'calling out' and is used to refer to an 'assembly, meeting, community, congregation, church, or society.'"[3] All who become followers of Christ have therefore a special calling from God to live in fidelity to God's purposes in ways that peculiarly identify them as God's people. Images that informed that sense of peculiar calling for the people called Christians came directly and powerfully from the images depicted in the Gospels of Jesus' calling of the disciples. In the worlds of Roman and Jewish cultures, Christians were to be a particular people called out to be faithful followers of Christ in the world.

In the process of assimilation of the Christian community into the Roman Empire involving the adoption of the Christian faith as the official religion of the Empire of Constantine, this communal meaning of calling or vocation underwent significant change. The meaning of calling was taken over by the clergy. Only those dedicating their lives to full-time, ordained ministry in the church could claim a Christian vocation, the only exception in the early centuries of Christianity being "when the dignity and sanction of a divine calling could be claimed for the emperor."[4] So excessive was this clerical dominance in the meaning of Christian vocation during the medieval period that it was the monastic life that came to signify the truest fulfillment of a calling to the religious life of devotion. As Fowler puts it succinctly, "Ordinary Christians could of course be saved, but only bishops, priests, and monks had callings."[5]

One does not have to reflect very long about the climate of separation between the clergy and the laity in most contemporary institutional expressions of Christianity to recognize that echoes of this understanding of divine calling being reserved primarily for the ordained are still present. The notion that persons are called to full-time Christian service but that ordinary persons choose their occupation is still very much alive in the meaning worlds of the contemporary church. To be sure, there are also present in the Christian community significant efforts to recover the meaning of Christian vocation in the ordinary work-a-day world. Nevertheless, it is frequently the case that God's involvement in calling persons to God's service is seen as having most often to do with a call to ordained or otherwise officially recognized religious ministry.

It is against this medieval mindset—with regard to the meaning of calling or vocation—that great Reformer, Martin Luther, took radical exception. For Luther, the call of followers of Christ to a life of Christian vocation was a call to a life of service to one's neighbor in whatever situation of life and work in which persons might find themselves. For Luther, therefore, the private life of devotion exercised in the seclusion of the monastery, rather than being the exercise of a vocational calling, represented an effort to justify oneself before God by one's works of devotion that ignored the call of God to concern for one's neighbor. True vocation was to be found in the day-to-day activities of the human community in the world, said Luther.

> A vocation is a "station" which is by nature helpful to others if it be followed. It is important to emphasize the fact that vocation is not confined to an occupation, but includes also what Betcke calls biological orders: father, mother, son, daughter. Every attempt to differentiate between the sphere of the home, where personal Christian love rules, and the sphere of office, where the more impersonal rules of vocation hold sway, immediately runs afoul of Luther's terminology. The life of the home, the relation between parents and children, is vocation, even as is life in the field of labor, the relation between employer and employee. In anything that involves action, anything that concerns the world or my relationship with my neighbor, there is nothing . . . that falls in a private sphere lying outside of station, office, or vocation. It is only before God, i.e., in heaven, that the individual stands alone. In the earthly realm [the human] always stands *in relatione*, always bound to another.[6]

Thus, for Luther, to exercise a vocation meant to take a certain stance toward the whole of life, both public and private, the stance of loving concern for those to whom one is related. It is as that concern permeates every level of relationship, from the most intimate to the most public and impersonal, that the calling to Christian vocation is fulfilled. Furthermore, it is love born of faith and the Spirit that "effects a complete breakthrough of the boundary between the two kingdoms, the wall of partition between heaven and earth, as did God's incarnation in Christ."[7] It is in the affirmation of the possibility of this breakthrough that Luther found the authorization for his often quoted declaration that the followers of Christ were to be "little Christs to one another."

Luther was quick to point out that the world of relationships within which one's vocation is to be realized is not the same for all people. The same course of action does not fit all circumstances. To fulfill Christian vocation does not always mean to do the same thing. Each person is to do his or her own work "without eyeing others or trying to copy them. Christ is not to be imitated by us, but rather to be accepted in faith, because Christ also has his special office for the salvation of [persons], an office which no one else has."[8]

Along with his emphasis upon the particularity of each individual's vocation unduplicated in the vocation of any other, Luther also placed heavy emphasis on the particularity of vocation in relation to time and circumstance. Each occasion thus calls for particular discernment of the call of God hidden in that occasion.

Since God is at work in the world about us, it is God who gives us the moment together with the relationships with others in our situation which the moment brings; and with these relationships [God] gives us our definite tasks. To use the moment and the time which God gives is to enter into one's vocation. It is in this way that what God ordains for "the time" is realized.[9]

We see that in the mind of Martin Luther there was a close link between human vocation and what might be spoken of as the vocation of God. The divine purpose in creation involves the exercise of God's creative powers in the fulfillment of God's promises within the created universe. Human vocation is found in its correspondence with the vocation of God as humans carry out the tasks of the time that God gives us. Thus, our human vocation is fulfilled as it is lived within the structure of God's vocation.

Over the centuries since Martin Luther took the meaning of the call to Christian vocation away from the ideal of the cloistered life of the monastery and toward life in the world and full participation of all persons in the work of the earthly kingdom, the meanings attached to vocation in Western culture have continued to evolve. Luther's turn toward the world was gradually transformed in its common-sense meaning by the end of the nineteenth century in such a way as to define vocation as simply having to do with any form of work by means of which persons earned wages or otherwise were provided a living. The coming of the industrial revolution undoubtedly hastened this process, what with its requirement of a wide variety of technical skills and the exercise of bodies of specialized knowledge. To have a vocation gradually took on the completely secularized meaning related to job, skill, or the practice of a profession. Vocational training, vocational education, and vocational guidance developed as fully secular activities designed to assist persons in making vocational choices and securing the training necessary to realize those vocational careers.

In the meantime, the meaning of calling in common usage has likewise undergone changes, although the sharp clarity of the shift toward secularity is less apparent than is the case with the popular usage of vocation. Dictionary definitions tend to include statements about usage as synonymous with vocational occupation or profession. They also include meanings such as "an inner urging toward some profession or activity."[10] Evidence can be seen of the movement within popular culture away from notions of calling as emanating from God toward the autonomy of human inner urging. Popular usage, particularly among Christians, however, has retained, albeit in only faintly articulate theological meaning, some sense

147

of summons or initiation from God toward the fulfillment of divine purpose in one's vocation. As stated earlier, the echoes of the medieval confinement of the meaning of calling to vocations of ordained ministry are most apparent. While particularly devout lay persons may in their own minds experience a calling to a particular profession or vocational activity, or struggle with the question as to whether or not what they are doing or planning to do is in accordance with God's call, in the more public sense to a large extent only the clergy are considered to have access to a special call to God's service.

One further shift in the common public meaning of work or vocation between the time of Martin Luther and the present needs to be underlined. It is imaged most clearly in the difference between what Luther referred to as station in the paragraph from Wingren's work on Luther quoted earlier and the taken-for-granted meaning of the term *vocational choice* in contemporary usage. In medieval times, and still to a great extent in the time of Luther, one did not choose what work or class status one enjoyed or suffered within. Rather, one's status was generally thought to be given by virtue of the status into which one was born. Luther's affirmation of the notion that persons were simply given a station in life by the mysterious action of God's grace was undoubtedly colored by this social practice of his time. On the other hand, our own time in American culture is strongly colored by taken-for-granted cultural appropriation of notions of individualism discussed earlier in chapter 1. Even though it is increasingly being recognized that, because of economic factors, cultural deprivations, and privileges of all kinds, all of which bring variation in opportunity, the degree of so-called free choice a person may enjoy varies enormously, the common-sense climate of assumption in America is rooted in images of individual choice and freedom to move from one status to another.

THE EMERGENCE OF CONTRACTUAL METAPHORS CONCERNING VOCATION

Relative to the purposes of this book, the principal outcome of this all too sketchy historical analysis of alterations in the meanings of vocation and calling is the recognition of the movement toward secularization and individualization. As the meaning of vocation has become more and more detached from images of a call emanating from God's gracious purpose in the sense that Luther understood it, the meaning of vocation in the world of public affairs has been drained of much of its fundamentally religious connotation. To have a vocation has therefore come to mean to have a job, a profession, or work to do in the world that fulfills either an individual or a corporate human purpose, or, in the best circumstances, both. In other words, the exercise of a vocation has become simply the fulfillment of a social contract between the individual and some aspect of the corporate society. To be sure, for some individuals and, indeed, for some social institutions, most often in the human services fields, a purpose understood as emanating from identifiable religious motivation or purpose may be at least implicitly written into the contract, but that is a matter for negotiation and contractual agreement.

Although it is beyond the purpose of this writing to engage in a full and detailed analysis of social contract theory, it will prove illuminating to uncover certain key aspects of the phenomenology of meanings that term has come to embody in its common-sense usage, particularly as those meanings relate to the implicit norms for human relationships that the image of contract has come to contain.

The use of the image of contract is both very old and thoroughly modern in human history. It is old because it had its beginnings in the earliest human need for exchange. Thus the simplest and perhaps earliest contract, one which is still a part of daily human interchange, was probably the result of a situation occurring when one person had something the other wanted and the second had something he or she was willing to give in exchange. The *quid pro quo* barter took place and the contract was fulfilled. Thus, a certain normative principle developed that became implicit in all contracts, the norm of equity, of so-called fair exchange.

It was this normative principle of *quid pro quo* that provided the parabolic twist to the story in the parable of Jesus known most often as the parable of the laborers and the hours. The wrenching parabolic shift of assumed reality in that parable comes when the *quid pro quo* principle is violated. Those who came to work toward the end of the day are paid the same as those who made a contractual bargain at the beginning of the day. The contractual normative expectation has been set aside in the service of a larger purpose. The action of the vineyard keeper seems on the face of it inequitable!

Our common-sense expectation as we read the parable reveals our taken-for-granted acceptance of the normative power of self-interest. Our automatic common-sense response to the story of the parable is to think that those who came to work early were either foolish or were cheated. They should have come later in the day and thus driven a better bargain for themselves or else the vineyard keeper should have paid them more! So half hidden in the common-sense understanding of contract is the notion that each is expected to look out for his or her own best interests. If all human exchange is a form of barter, each is expected to get as much as one can while giving as little as possible or necessary, though admittedly, other motivations may begin to enter the situation when some larger purpose comes into play, as, we may suppose, was the case with the vineyard keeper. With one's spouse or one's child or parent, particularly, and even with one's friends and acquaintances, a certain concern for the other most often skews the straight-forward bargaining posture implied in the contract imagery.

Contracts also contain the imagery of forethought or anticipation. To enter into a contract most often expresses a common intentionality that is to be made binding on the parties to the contract. Contracts are entered into prior to action, in anticipation of possible, even perhaps inevitable difficulties. In a sense, they are intended to govern anticipation. One can expect only what the other has contracted to provide or perform. They are negotiated, in part, to set controls and limits ahead of time on how difficulties are to be managed and expectations limited. That means also that contracts provide a certain legitimization for calling the other into account and, in turn, being called into account by the other. Have you lived up to your bargain? If not, some retribution may, according to the image of contract, be expected.

Finally, in the modern world that has come to highly value individualism and autonomy, the contractual mode of human relationships has come to mean a temporary structure of relationship that can be broken or terminated should one's participation in the contracted relationship prove undesirable or difficult. We have come to expect contracts, including even marriage contracts and the contractual obligations of parenthood, to be broken or ended if they prove to be dissatisfying or too costly to the felt needs of the self. Said perhaps a bit crassly, our culture has come to the point of affirmation of the right to look for a better deal, a stance in many respects quite the opposite of Martin Luther's notion of station.

One of the important arguments of this book has to do with the analagous nature of the situation in the church's commonly held understanding of its relationship to the world in our time resulting from the privatization of religious expression to the time when Martin Luther sought to turn the meaning of Christian vocation away from the monastery toward the broad arena of human relationships in the world. As Luther came to argue that the monastic tradition had become too concerned with its own salvation, so it seems in our time that the privatization of religious life and vocation has resulted in the

150

preoccupation of the church and church people with their own salvific well-being and seclusion of the church and its people from the larger arena of life and work in the world. As Luther sought to recover the meaning of Christian vocation in relation to family life, labor in one's occupation, and public affairs, so we in the church need to recover the implications of God's call into Christian vocation in relation to each and every aspect of human affairs.

For those of us in pastoral ministry who have participated in the modern preoccupation of pastoral care with the care of persons in their so-called private relationships, and thereby have participated in unanticipated ways in the cultural thrust toward self preoccupation, the realization that our care may have unwittingly encouraged this turn toward privatization of vocation may come as a word of judgment. It is a word of wisdom from the past of our tradition that reminds us that it is not enough to assist people in their efforts to extract a better, more equitable and self-fulfilling contract from their human relationships. It is a reminder that the God who set us in this place in the conditions in which we are located has thereby graciously given us, as well as those to whom we minister, a call to exercise our Christian vocation in all of the arenas of human relationship in which we are involved in the world.

TOWARD THE RECOVERY
OF COVENANTAL METAPHORS OF VOCATION

Set over against and in dialectical tension with the appropriation of contractual images of human transactional relationships are those images that spring from the ancient biblical tradition of covenant, the metaphor that appears again and again in the Bible that governs the relationship of Yahweh with Yahweh's people. In the biblical tradition, human relationships are to be modeled after that inclusive covenant between God and human beings.[11] If Christians are to recover Martin Luther's interpretation of the biblical tradition's linkage between the images of calling from God and our vocation, we will do so in large part by the recovery of the traditional image of covenant.

In considering the implications of the recovery of covenantal imagery in relation to pastoral work, I am particularly indebted to my now retired former colleague and Professor of Religion at Emory University, William A. Beardslee. A teacher of New Testament with particular interest in the relationship between the interpretation of scripture and process philosophical thought, Beardslee some years ago shared with his faculty colleagues an unpublished paper titled, "Marriage as Covenant: Some

Biblical and Theological Reflections.'"[12] Although that paper is specifically concerned with issues related to the incursion of contractual models into the way the marital relationship is imaged in Western culture, his understanding of the covenantal tradition has much wider applicability in relation to all metaphorical construction of human relationships.

Beardslee begins his consideration of contemporary marriage patterns by pointing to the primacy of the problem of continuity. He accepts the fact that in our increasingly secularized society we can no longer expect that the Christian normative vision of the life-long continuity of marriage will be the societal standard. Rather, that paradigmatic model, poetically expressed in the traditional marriage vows—richer or poorer, in sickness and in health, 'til death do us part—may become a minority view that will indeed be replaced by more contractual, terminable expectation patterns.

In certain ways, Beardslee suggests, this is not vastly different from the situation in later Old Testament and New Testament times. Whereas the larger society held the value of continuity in marriage commitments rather loosely, that value was given much stronger emphasis in both the devout Jewish and the early Christian communities. Beardslee reminds his readers, however, that these tight restrictions on divorce among Christians were set in the midst of the imminent expectation of the radical transformation of all human existence with the coming of the *eschaton*. A new covenant was in process of coming into being. Until that time, Paul and other Christian leaders stood for keeping all relationships as stable as possible.

Beardslee indicates, as does virtually all contemporary biblical scholarship, that in the Hebrew scriptures covenant was, first and foremost, a metaphor used to describe the relation between the people of Israel and God.[13] Like most biblical imagery concerning God and the God-human relationship, the covenantal metaphor was drawn from an analogy in the experience of the early Israelite people, namely, its use in political treaties handed down by a great king to his vassals. The covenant of God with Israel, remembered from the experiences of Sinai and from Shechem, was considered to be an agreement between God and God's people. It was not, however, an equal agreement. God took the initiative and it was up to the people to keep the agreement as it was up to God to keep the promises to the people contained in the agreement. Thus, life in the covenant became life under the claim of One who was far beyond the daily affairs of persons, yet who was deeply involved in and concerned about those persons and their affairs.

Beardslee points to three aspects of the covenant image as it developed across the years of biblical times. First, there developed fixed formulas, as classically modeled in the Ten Commandments, by which the people were expected to govern their participation in the life of covenant. These formulas had both the purpose of regulation and of prediction, that is, to state in advance what is demanded by agreement. In this aspect, it may be said that the covenantal tradition contains some of the elements that were precursors of modern images of contract. Stated in traditional theological terms, here is to be found the aspect of law in the covenant tradition.

A second aspect of speech about the covenant Beardslee delineates is that of the story connected with it.

> The great story of the Exodus and its continuation into the settlement of the land offers a context for the covenant at Sinai, a context which interprets the kind of claim made upon the Hebrews by showing that their story is a story of interaction with a particular kind of God. In a word, the commandments clarify the covenant as demand; the story clarifies the covenant as gift. It shows how unexpected, undeserved, and surprising the whole existence of the people was.[14]

Reflection on this aspect of the covenant tradition brings to the fore the importance of the element of risk in that image. To be a covenant people meant taking chances, venturing into the unknown. For God, it meant risking the free actions and decisions of the people and commitment to be the people's God in all the ups and downs of the story that emerged from their life together. We begin to see that, whereas the image of contract contains the desire to reduce risk through *quid pro quo* requirements, the image of covenant brings into tension with that desire the element of promise, both in terms of willingness to risk and the expectation of fulfillment beyond what is now present.

Beardslee points to a third element in the Hebrew image of covenant that emerged from the very different covenant God made with David from that made with Israel as a whole. Foreshadowed by the earlier covenants with Noah and with Abraham, this covenant did not specify any human requirements to be met if the covenant was to be valid. It rather represented an outright divine gift of promise in a totally one-sided fashion. Here again enters a tension with the *quid pro quo* of contractual imagery. In covenantal relationships, gifts may be freely offered without expectation of return. It could be expected to enter another arena beyond the arena of barter and self-interest.

So the biblical portrait of the earliest beginnings of the covenantal tradition emerges as a peculiarly strange mixture of contract: the expectation that human relationships will be governed by aspects of law guaranteeing the fulfillment of promised expectations, and gift: the giving of self to the other in ways not expected or demanded by agreement. Those two sides of covenant are then enclosed within a story of a people and their God who together confront all of the vicissitudes of changing times, changing situations, changing needs, dilemmas, and opportunities. More than a contract, the biblical image of covenant signifies life together in commitment to the welfare of one another and the purposes of the One who first formed the people of God into a covenant community. The story of that biblical people is thus a story of success and failure, the gradual expansion of their understanding of their communal vocation toward their becoming "a light to the nations," coupled with the persistence of their failure to live up to that vision.

If we who form the Christian community and its pastoral leadership today are to learn from the wisdom of the biblical covenantal tradition and from the great Reformer who turned the vision of vocation of the medieval church out of its cloistered monastic sanctuary into life in the world lived under the calling of God, it may be said that our vocation as Christians will likewise be found in the reformulation and reinterpretation of the meaning of life together as a people of the covenant. We will be called out of our self preoccupations into the wider arenas of life together with all the peoples of the earth. And we will be called to confront our failures, our petty preoccupations with our own comfort, our own survival as a community of affluence and upward mobility.

COMPLICATIONS OF A COVENANTAL VISION

Having agreed that the individual and corporate vocation of the Christian community toward which God is calling us is to be realized out in the world, ordinary American Christians will be immediately confronted with a situation of seemingly insurmountable complications. Those complications will present themselves in multiform ways in all locations both near at hand and remote from our immediate community of faith and practice. To imagine seeking to be a people present in the world as representatives of a vision of life together informed by the images of care for the other in ways that are covenantal runs hard against very basic common-sense understandings of how both the private and the public worlds function.

Although most of these complications are so common among most Americans that they supply the content of much of the daily conversation that goes on in households and among friends and acquaintances, it seems useful to categorize and list them. Taken together, they make up a socio-cultural situation of great complexity.

154

1. First, and perhaps most closely at hand, such a vision of Christian vocation will encounter the complication of the necessity of a pluralism of commitments and functional roles on the part of most, if not all, members of the Christian community.

As the modern world functions, individuals are called upon to fulfill a wide variety of social roles, each having its own set of priorities, purposes, and life-complicating problems. Typically such roles will include those of spouse and parent, member of some community of persons involved in the work of the world, citizen of one or more governmental/political communities, and participant in a local, as well as broader, community of faith, to name but a few of the long list of social roles into which persons may enter. To be fully and actively present in each of these roles in ways that respond to the calling to Christian vocation envisioned in the foregoing paragraphs seems on the face of it very difficult indeed, if not an impossibility. Problems of prioritizing role relationships, commitments of time and energy, responses to needs and expectations can become so complicated as to seem unmanageable. Furthermore, in each of those social roles persons will, if they become sensitized to the commonly held assumptions and construals of those roles, find conflicting values, norms, and visions of how that role is best fulfilled. In such a situation it becomes exceedingly difficult for the ordinary Christian to experience anything approaching a single-minded sense of vocation.

Patricia Johnson is but one example of a person experiencing this level of complication in her life. Nominally reared in a mainline Protestant home as an only child in a family in which her father was, for most of her adolescence, a home-bound invalid and her mother a full-time breadwinner and part-time nurse to her husband, Patricia learned early in life to fend for herself. She also learned that, in ways she came to understand only much later through a psychotherapeutic relationship, the welfare of her parents as persons was peculiarly her responsibility.

After college, Patricia became a school teacher and, some years later, married. Now in her middle years, she finds herself a mother of an active and precocious four-year-old daughter and the operating partner in a family business she owns with her husband. The husband's involvement in the business is largely as financial manager and entrepreneur; Patricia runs the day-to-day operations of the business. Patricia's mother, now in her late seventies and living alone near her

155

daughter, has become more and more deeply dependent on Patricia for everything from rides to the shopping center to emotional support in her loneliness.

As an employer of a staff of some fifty people in the family business, Patricia has the role of personnel manager and trainer of a seemingly constant procession of relatively short-term employees. She and her husband also dabble in county politics, a role Patricia both enjoys and deplores because of the social demands it entails. In recent years, they have, with the coming of their child, renewed a once dormant relationship with the church after months of shopping around for a compatible community of faith in which they could feel at home.

Such a relatively simple narrative of Patricia Johnson's role relationship involvements fails to do justice to the complications she experiences as she seeks to live a life of authentic, responsible personhood. The qualities of presence required of her by her multiple roles are both varied and, from her perspective, often conflicting. Demands of her role as businesswoman—a role she not only sees as necessary, but also enjoys—have required that she make use of a nearby day care center and nursery school for the care of her child during the busiest hours of the day. She often feels both guilty and deprived that she is not being a full-time mother. She worries about whether her daughter is receiving the quality of care she could provide if she didn't have to be a working mother. Often at the end of the working day, when she does have time for her child, she finds herself too tired to give her daughter the attention both of them would like. Yet, her work in the business seems both necessary and rewarding. And what to do about mother, particularly in the years just ahead, when from all indications mother will be increasingly unable to care for herself? Move her into the family home? Encourage her to move into a senior citizens' complex, something mother is dead set against at this point?

Patricia also worries about how to balance her deep-seated inclination to become personally involved in caring for her employees with the profit and loss requirements of the business that she deal with them impersonally. In the latter role she finds herself needing to be objective and managerial, demanding adequate performance of required work and weeding out those who fail to live up to her expectations. Strict adherence to contractual expectations competes repeatedly with covenantal modes of caring for her workers in those relationships.

The situation in which Patricia Johnson finds herself can be found with infinite variation all across American society. It is a situation in which both men and women participate, although in a time of societal transition with regard to common-sense understandings of the roles of women, the greater burden of multiple roles seems clearly to be carried by them. For individuals caught up in the complexities such life situations entail, the effort involved in fulfilling one's Christian vocation in and through a certain mode of presence and covenantally shaped set of communal relationships becomes exceedingly complicated.

2. A second set of complications, closely related to and often hidden within the first, might be described as the complications resulting from conflicts between the worldly wisdom of American societal practices and the covenantal wisdom of the biblical tradition.

We encounter once again the extent to which broad areas of cultural life tend to be governed by the rule of common-sense understandings of how society operates. Over time, every society builds up a largely unwritten code of such common sense practical wisdom. Furthermore, each facet or segment of the society, be it an organized political party, a business operation, or a professional guild, on the one hand, or an informal race or class status group, on the other, accumulates a tradition of lore into which participants in that facet of societal life are socialized. In often subtle ways, participants are encouraged to take for granted those worldly-wise rules and reasons as being true for that activity and/or for that group's relationship to society as a whole.

Such worldly wisdom has, to be sure, played an important role in organizing and sustaining cultural practices since early biblical times. The inclusion of the Book of Proverbs in the Hebrew canon attests to its place in the history of cultural practical religious wisdom. In the modern context, the body of such lore concerning how the world operates has undoubtedly become more highly particularized and diverse. Yet its rule of ordinary human affairs remains pervasive.

Among the many ways in which pastors have encountered certain of the complications worldly wisdom creates in the affairs of the church have been the complications resulting from the intrusion of the worldly wisdom of the business world into the conduct of the affairs of the local congregation. More than one businessman church leader has sought to make the decision making and financial operations of the church "more like we do it in the business world." Sometimes the results are salutary in that the financial affairs of the congregation become more orderly and accountable. Often, however, the promotional, sales-oriented lore of business can so intrude on the life of the congregation that, for example,

157

the annual necessity to underwrite the budget of the church can take on the atmosphere of a marketing campaign that threatens to supersede in the consciousness of the participants in the process any awareness of the congregation as a covenantal community whose presence in the world is to be an alternative to the cultural norm of that society.

3. Third, hidden within the two sets of complications already listed lies a set of complications for the fulfillment of individual and corporate vocation as calling from God brought about because we who seek to find our narrative home within the Christian story of the world must also live within numerous other narrative structures that compete in the shaping of our cultural life.

Furthermore, we live in a world grown small and fraught with the growing realization of the pluralism of religious and secular traditions, the pluralism of cultures.

Much as we who claim the Christian story of the world as our normative narrative—within which we seek to nest all of the little stories of our lives—may wish that all of the peoples of the world could share our Christian narrative understanding, we are in our time bombarded with evidence that this is not the case even in North America, to say nothing of the rest of the world. We are thus confronted with the complicated realization that our Christian understanding of the world—an understanding that our tradition has shaped through time and history—is but one way of construing the world and life in the world.

This realization that is gradually settling upon the Christian community brings complications to the realization of our God-given vocation in two important ways. First, it brings the complicating awareness that the Christian story is not the only narrative of how the world is and how it operates in which we participate in our common life. Rather, we participate in numerous stories, some scientific and supposedly empirically verifiable, such as the story we enter into every time we go to a medical clinic or hospital. Some of the stories of our lives are more visibly aesthetic or mythical, such as those in which we participate when we listen to a great symphony or a rock band. Some supposedly are very down to earth and practical, such as the common-sense story of how to get along in a particular neighborhood or part of the country. So we are confronted with all of the complications involved in participating in this multitude of narratives of the world while yet claiming our Christian vocation as the bedrock organizing and decision-making normative vision for our living.

The second complication this realization of a pluralism of narratives creates comes with the realization that there are other religious traditions with differing stories of the world that not only shape a construal of life in the world that are different from the Christian tradition's construal of it, but also may raise questions or present alternative ways of seeing things in the world that are potentially significant for those of us who identify ourselves as Christians.

The example that speaks most clearly to me from recent experience comes from an encounter with a wise and articulate native American who is both a Christian and a scholar of the historic faith of the native people of the American West. In speaking to a group of Christian pastoral theologians, this person spoke with deep conviction and gentle power of his people's way of construing the relationship between humans and the physical environment. Native Americans, he said, never have seen themselves as the masters of their physical world, but as participants in it along with the other creatures of the earth. He spoke of their reverence for Nature and of the white man's compelling need to subdue the earth. For him, the covenantal relationship between humans and the natural world was primary in ways that sees life itself as a gift from the natural world. Nature cares for its creatures as its human creatures are expected to care for nature. He spoke with deep anger about the plundering of both the natural world and his people by the white society informed by the dominant Christian religion of the West.

Such encounters greatly complicate and relativize our European-American appropriation of the Judeo-Christian covenantal tradition. They come as a judgment on our commonly accepted certainties about what the God-given Christian vocation is and should be. The "otherness" of these non-Christian traditions can speak a prophetic word to us concerning our own tradition and vocation.

4. Fourth is complications in the fulfillment of both individual and corporate vocation brought about by the difficulties involved in the making and breaking of covenants in modern life.

As was noted earlier, in William Beardslee's analysis of the implications of the biblical covenantal tradition in relation to marriage, his initial concern with regard to marriage in the modern context had to do with the problem of continuity in a cultural situation in which temporariness has increasingly become the standard rather than the exception. How is it possible to sustain the continuity of a covenantal vocation in marriage—a standard that the Christian understanding of marriage clearly upholds—when the culture in which we find ourselves no longer seems to support that standard? Yet the longing for a marriage relationship that fulfills the desire and expectation of a deeply committed, essentially covenantal relationship with a spouse as primary vocational partner persists. For most Americans, it is the relationship that most clearly contains the deepest desires and hopes for a sustained and sustaining relationship of continuity and commitments.[15]

While the vision of a vocation-fulfilling, covenantal marital relationship does indeed remain strong in American life, evidence mounts that the difficulties and complications in forming such relationships—and sustaining them once they are established—has greatly increased in the modern situation. Postponement of marriage, temporary liaisons between unmarried partners, intentional and unintentional single life-styles, serial monogamy, and divorce abound in American society among Christians and non-Christians alike. If relationships between the sexes are taken as an indicator, it seems clear that Americans are experiencing the making and breaking of covenantal relationships as exceedingly complicated!

Complex and difficult as is that set of complications with regard to making and sustaining covenants, it is not the only arena of modern life where these complications may be found. Something similar is happening in the American workplace. Temporariness, limited and purely instrumental commitments, exploitation, and survivalism seem, in many sectors of the working world, to be the rule rather than the exception. The number of persons who go to work for an employer, work for thirty to forty years for the same employer, and then retire on that company's pension decreases year by year, while the number of people who experience their working life as a series of short term, contingent, and expedient job relationships increases. Meanwhile, the sense of being in a covenantal relationship with one's fellow workers and one's employer tends to diminish, if not disappear entirely.

This condition of temporariness and expediency is nowhere greater than in the so-called service industries that provide the fast food and cloned consumer goods that fill the suburban malls and that line an increasing number of highways into small-town America. Low pay, high turnover in employees among labor and management, and low levels of continuity and commitment are increasingly accepted as expected in these activities that support America's fast growing, fast moving, "use it up and throw it away" marketplace. Where in this milieu can covenantal images of vocation flourish?

National television news recently reported one small effort to respond creatively to this unhappy and unprofitable situation of temporary, low-level commitment to sustaining relationships in the fast food industry. It seems a very imaginative owner/manager of a fast food hamburger chain franchise decided to do something about the poor motivation among his employees. He was also concerned about their penchant to move from job to job just when he had them trained to give the desired service to his customers. He initiated a program in which he covenanted with his employees to provide them full tuition and books for any recognized educational program that would help them to advance their competence in some chosen field. In return, the employees were asked to agree to stay with him until their educational goals were realized. Somewhat to his amazement, the turnover rate decreased virtually to zero over periods of up to four years or longer. His employees became a closely knit working group who took corporate pride in their work. Their relationships with customers improved markedly. Thus, a fast-food fast-turnover place became a microcenter of nourishing, hopeful, and helpful relationships. Furthermore, his costs for training were greatly reduced and his profit margin grew substantially!

However, for literally thousands of Americans today, the complications involved in sustaining a sense of meaningful vocation within a family or working community held together by a covenant are difficult to calculate, let alone to transform. Many factors combine to present difficulties at the point of making significant covenantal relationships. Also, difficulties arise when encountering the vicissitudes of sustaining such relationships as they are bombarded by the complexities of modern life, and, then, when that becomes impossible—out of necessity—breaking them.

THE ELUSIVE PRESENCE OF THE CHRISTIAN COMMUNITY

It is in response to this general situation of great complexity and difficulty with regard to the realization of a meaningful, caring, and sustaining sense of vocation among all the peoples of the world that the Christian community and its people must find their particular vocation in the world in which we live. It is not a vocation that can be found within the secluded privacy of that community's own life, though that life should seek to become an exemplar of what it means to be a people of the covenant. Rather, the Christian community's vocation will be realized, and God's call to God's people will find appropriate response, as ways are found to provide a leavening presence in all the places where human beings are together. As the centrifugal model of the church discussed in the previous chapter suggests, the church's true vocation will be found not so much as it draws the world to itself, but as it dislocates itself into the world as a servant people to "be a light to the nations."

Just here it is important that the Christian community and its individual

161

PROPHETIC PASTORAL PRACTICE

members seek imaginatively to appropriate the realization concerning the presence of God and God's calling that came to the people of the Bible to which I referred in an earlier chapter as the realization of the "elusive presence of God" among them. God' s presence and God's call of the people of the Bible to their vocation was never a matter under their control and it came to them often in hidden, elusive ways. It seldom came as they expected it, or with great fanfare. Hidden in a burning bush or a still small voice, the call of God as often as not came quietly only to those "who had eyes to see and ears to hear." Furthermore, as was said earlier, the presence of the people of God was to be modeled after God's presence.

Does this not suggest that the vocational presence of the self-identified community of God's people will most often be a quiet, elusive presence, rather than one that is loud and commanding? Does it not suggest that even the language of Christian vocation may most appropriately at times be hidden within other ways of speaking about what is needed wherever and whenever human beings seek new and more caring ways of being together? To be sure, it is equally crucial that the people called Christian keep ever renewed the ties to their own story of the world, the language that tells them of the care of God for God's people. But, just as God's presence in human affairs is, according to that story, most often elusive and hidden, so the leaven of Christian vocation will in most situations be an elusive, hidden presence more concerned with the transformation of the whole of human life than with its own public acknowledgment.

THE VOCATION OF THE CHRISTIAN PASTOR

And so we come to the end of this effort to explore an imaginative, metaphorical approach to practical theological reflection on the recovery of a normative vision of life together and the role of the Christian community in the transformation of the common-sense culture of our time. Coming to the end, I am made aware once again of the enormity of such an undertaking. The power of the common sense culture to control human relationships is so pervasive and taken for granted, that to think of seeking to transform its ways seems a foolish and naive undertaking.

Yes, I have argued on these pages that in our time it is to just such a vocation that the deepest themes of the story of our tradition are calling Christian people. The fragmentation and confusion abroad among the people of the modern world with regard to norms, boundaries, and visions of the good and humanly desirable life contain both the pain of

162

the people to which we are called to respond, and the half-hidden opportunity for offering a transformative possibility. The signs of the times point to the pain of the problem and the cracks in the facade of common-sense culture through which the deep wisdom of our faith tradition may, if imaginatively and prophetically presented, enter.

I have also argued that both the Christian pastor and layperson, because of her or his unique location close at hand to the ordinary, everyday life of the people has thereby a peculiar and significant access both to the ways in which common sense functions in the daily life of the people and to those large and small occurrences that interrupt the flow of common-sense rule of ordinary life. It is in the signals of suffering and confusion that accompany those interruptions that the sensitive ministry practitioner may hear the cry for transformation of the people and the call of God to prophetic ministry.

In lifting up for attention and practical theological reflection this dimension of ordinariness in the life of any community, I am joined by Walter Brueggemann, who, in the last chapter of his *Prophetic Imagination*, says:

> Prophetic ministry does not consist of spectacular acts of social crusading or of abrasive measures of indignation. Rather, prophetic ministry consists of offering an alternative perception of reality and letting people see their own history in the light of God's freedom and (God's) will for justice. . . . The practice of prophetic ministry is not some special thing done two days a week. Rather, it is done in, with, and under all the acts of ministry—as much in counseling as in preaching, as much in liturgy as in education. It concerns a stance and posture or a hermeneutic about the world of death and the word of life that can be brought to light in every context.[16]

I would only add to what Brueggemann has said that prophetic ministry involves the conjoining of the pastor's interpretive guidance role in the center of the identified Christian community as schematized in the centripetal model of the church and the pastor's role as caring, inquiring, and sometimes guiding symbolic figure in all the dislocations from that identified community out in the world where the whole people of God may be found, as schematized in the centrifugal model.

In sum, the minister's role in fulfilling the calling of God to a transformative vocation for the Christian people in the world is a pastorally prophetic role. The most excellent and faithful expression of that role combines the best of the pastoral tradition—with its sensitivity to human need, human frailty, and caughtness in deception, and the best of the prophetic tradition—with its concern for justice, awareness of systemic evil and dominance over persons, and its eschatological vision of that reality toward which God is calling the human community. In its most imaginative expression, the fulfillment of that role makes use of image, metaphor, and story, the thematic and aesthetic wisdom of the tradition to which it seeks to be loyal. In its most hopeful expression, persons living out that role keep before them the eschatological vision of that Kingdom in which all things shall be made new and all the people shall dwell in the fullness of the knowledge of God.

If this be the vocation to which God is calling those of us who are pastoral leaders of Christian communities, then we have this assurance: To those whom God calls, God will be faithful. That is the central theme of the story of our faith.

NOTES

Introduction: Responding Pastorally to the Signs of the Times

1. Charles V. Gerkin, *Widening the Horizons: Pastoral Responses to a Fragmented Society* (Philadelphia: Westminster Press, 1986).
2. Robert Bellah, Richard Madsen, William M. Sullivan, Ann Swidler, and Steven M. Tipton, *Habits of the Heart: Individualism and Commitment in American Life* (Berkeley: University of California Press, 1985).
3. For an explication of Ricoeur's concept of the hermeneutic of suspicion, see Charles E. Reagan and David Stewart, eds., *The Philosophy of Paul Ricoeur* (Boston: Beacon Press, 1978), pp. 214, 215.
4. "There is no more an isolated horizon of the present than there are historical horizons. Understanding, rather, is always the fusion of these horizons which we imagine to exist by themselves. We know the power of this kind of fusion chiefly from earlier times and their naive attitude to themselves and their origin. In a tradition, this process of fusion is continually going on, for there old and new continually grow together to make something of living value, without either being explicitly distinguished from the other." (Hans-Georg Gadamer, *Truth and Method* [New York: Crossroad, 1982], p. 273.)
5. See the bibliography at the end of the book for a listing of the writings of Hans-Georg Gadamer and Paul Ricoeur that are particularly pertinent for the model being developed here. Gadamer's *Truth and Method* is specifically foundational for the development of the model.
6. For the development of an approach to practical theology based on the concept of practical moral reasoning, see Don S. Browning, *Religious Ethics and Pastoral Care* (Philadelphia: Fortress Press, 1983), and *Religious Thought and the Modern Psychologies* (Philadelphia: Fortress Press, 1987).
7. Sallie McFague, *Metaphorical Theology: Models of God in Religious Language* (Philadelphia: Fortress Press, 1982). *See also* David Tracy, *The Blessed Rage for Order* (New York: Seabury Press, Crossroad, 1975), and *The Analogical Imagination* (New York: Seabury Press, 1978).

1. Pastoral Care and the New Search for Norms

1. David Tracy, *Plurality and Ambiguity: Hermeneutics, Religion, Hope* (San Francisco: Harper & Row, 1987), p. 70.

2. Russell Jacoby, *Social Amnesia* (Boston: Beacon Press, 1975), p. 104.
3. Robert N. Bellah, Richard Madsen, William M. Sullivan, Ann Swidler, and Steven M. Tipton, *Habits of the Heart: Individualism and Commitment in American Life* (Berkeley: University of California Press, 1985). pp. 32, 33.
4. Ibid., pp. 143, 144.
5. E. Brooks Holifield, *A History of Pastoral Care in America: From Salvation to Self-Realization* (Nashville: Abingdon Press, 1983), p. 204. *See also* Allison Stokes, *Ministry After Freud* (New York: Pilgrim Press, 1985), p. 22.
6. William James, *The Varieties of Religious Experience* (Garden City, N.Y.: Doubleday Image Books, 1978).
7. Holifield, *A History of Pastoral Care in America*, pp. 259, 260.
8. A number of the humanistic psychologists could be cited as examples here. *See,* for example, Abraham Maslow, *The Farther Reaches of Human Nature* (New York: Viking Press, 1971), p. 15; Carl R. Rogers, *Client-Centered Therapy* (Boston: Houghton Mifflin Co., 1951, 1965), p. 488; Erich Fromm, *Man for Himself* (New York: Rinehart and Co., 1947), p. 7.
9. Philip Rieff, *The Triumph of the Therapeutic: Uses of Faith After Freud* (New York: Harper & Row, 1966).
10. James Melvin Washington, ed., *A Testament of Hope: The Essential Writings of Martin Luther King, Jr.* (San Francisco: Harper & Row, 1986), p. 119.
11. The term *classic* is used here in the sense in which it is used by the theologian David Tracy. *See,* for example, his *Analogical Imagination: Christian Theology and the Culture of Pluralism* (New York: Crossroad, 1986), p. 104; or "The Foundations of Practical Theology" in Don S. Browning, ed., *Practical Theology: The Emerging Field in Theology, Church, and World* (San Francisco: Harper & Row, 1983), p. 64.

    The list of feminist theologians who have, from various and somewhat differing perspectives, pressed for a radical critique of biblical and other classical Christian theology as pervaded by androcentrism and patriarchal modeling of core theological imagery, is too long to cite fully here. I have in mind the work of such prominent contemporary figures as Rosemary Radford Ruether (*Sexism and God-Talk: Toward a Feminist Theology* [Boston: Beacon Press, 1984]); Elisabeth Schüssler Fiorenza (*Bread Not Stone: The Challenge of Feminist Biblical Interpretation* [Boston: Beacon Press, 1986]); Phyllis Trible (*God and the Rhetoric of Sexuality* [Philadelphia: Fortress Press, 1978] and *Texts of Terror: Literary-Feminist Readings of Biblical Narratives* [Philadelphia: Fortress Press, 1984]); Catherine Keller (*From a Broken Web: Separation, Sexism, and Self* [Boston: Beacon Press, 1986]); and Sallie McFague (*Models of God: Theology for an Ecological, Nuclear Age* [Philadelphia: Fortress Press, 1987]).
12. Catherine Keller, *From a Broken Web: Separation, Sexism, and Self* (Boston: Beacon Press, 1986), p. 88.
13. Sallie McFague, *Models of God: Theology for an Ecological, Nuclear Age* (Philadelphia: Fortress Press, 1987), p. 21.
14. Carol Gilligan, *In a Different Voice* (Cambridge: Harvard University Press, 1982).
15. Charles V. Gerkin, *Widening the Horizons: Pastoral Responses to a Fragmented Society* (Philadelphia: Westminster Press, 1986), chap. 5.
16. Hans-Georg Gadamer, *Truth and Method* (New York: Crossroad, 1982), p. 271.
17. Phyllis Trible, *Texts of Terror: Literary-Feminist Readings of Biblical Narratives* (Philadelphia: Fortress Press, 1984), p. 3.
18. Gerkin, *Widening the Horizons*, p. 73.

2. By Reason or by the Imagination?

1. Don S. Browning, *Religious Ethics and Pastoral Care* (Philadelphia: Fortress Press, 1983), p. 16.
2. Johann Baptist Metz, *Faith in History and Society: Toward a Practical Fundamental Theology* (New York: Seabury Press, 1980), p. 35. *See also* Parker J. Palmer, *The Company*

of Strangers: Christians and the Renewal of America's Public Life (New York: Crossroad, 1985).

3. Ibid., p. 56.
4. Hans-Georg Gadamer, *Truth and Method* (New York: Crossroad, 1982), p. 31.
5. Ibid., p. 33.
6. Ibid., p. 36.
7. Donald A. Schon, *The Reflective Practitioner: How Professionals Think in Action* (New York: Basic Books, 1983), chap. 5.
8. Gadamer, *Truth and Method*, p. 36.
9. H. Richard Niebuhr, *The Responsible Self* (New York: Harper & Row, 1963), pp. 60-61.
10. Alan Richardson and John Bowden, eds., *The Westminster Dictionary of Christian Theology* (Philadelphia: Westminster Press, 1983), p. 323.
11. Niebuhr, *The Responsible Self*, p. 107.
12. Ibid., pp. 66, 67.
13. Ibid., p. 67.
14. Charles V. Gerkin, *The Living Human Document: Re-Visioning Pastoral Counseling in a Hermeneutical Mode* (Nashville: Abingdon Press, 1984).
15. Charles V. Gerkin, *Widening the Horizons: Pastoral Responses to a Fragmented Society* (Philadelphia: Westminster Press, 1986).
16. Gerkin, *The Living Human Document*, chap. 5.
17. Gerkin, *Widening the Horizons*, chaps. 2 and 3.
18. "To put it another way, time becomes human to the extent that it is articulated through a narrative mode, and narrative attains its full meaning when it becomes a condition of temporal existence." (Paul Ricoeur, *Time and Narrative*, vol. 1 [Chicago: University of Chicago Press, 1984], p. 52.)
19. Paul Ricoeur, *Time and Narrative*, vol. 3 (Chicago: University of Chicago Press, 1988), p. 185.
20. Ricoeur, *Time and Narrative*, vol. 3. *See* especially "Conclusions," pp. 241-74.
21. Ibid., p. 183.
22. Niebuhr, *The Responsible Self*, p. 67.
23. Gadamer, *Truth and Method*, p. 53.
24. Gerkin, *Widening the Horizons*, p. 61.

3. From Imagination to Metaphor

1. Charles V. Gerkin, *Widening the Horizons: Pastoral Responses to a Fragmented Society* (Philadelphia: Westminster Press, 1986), pp. 100-101.
2. Hans-Georg Gadamer, *Truth and Method* (New York: Crossroad, 1982), p. 37.
3. Ibid., p. 38.
4. Walter Brueggemann, *The Prophetic Imagination* (Philadelphia: Fortress Press, 1978), p. 12.
5. Ibid., p. 114.
6. Ibid., p. 13.
7. Ibid.
8. Howard Wall, "A Local Display of World Communion," p. 828. Copyright 1988, Christian Century Foundation. Reprinted by permission from the September 28, 1988, issue of *The Christian Century*.
9. Brueggemann, *The Prophetic Imagination*, p. 21.
10. Abraham Heschel, *The Prophets*, vol. 1 (New York: Harper & Row. Harper Torchbooks, 1969), p. 6. *See also* my reference to Heschel's interpretation of the prophets of Israel in *Widening the Horizons*, p. 93.
11. Wayne E. Oates, *Pastoral Counseling in Social Problems: Extremism, Race, Sex, Divorce* (Philadelphia: Westminster Press, 1966). *See also* his later *Pastoral Counseling* (Philadelphia: Westminster Press, 1974), pp. 164-66.
12. Howard Wall, "A Local Display of World Communion," pp. 829-30.

13. Mary Gerhart and Allan M. Russell, *Metaphoric Process: The Creation of Scientific and Religious Understanding* (Fort Worth: Texas Christian University Press, 1984), pp. 90-91. Gerhart and Russell utilize a conception of "themata" taken from the work of Gerald Holton in his book, *Thematic Origins of Scientific Thought* (Cambridge: Harvard University Press, 1973).
14. Ibid., p. 89.
15. Paul Ricoeur, *The Rule of Metaphor: Multi-disciplinary Studies of the Creation of Meaning in Language* (Toronto: University of Toronto Press, 1981), pp. 255-56.
16. For a further explication of the concept of fusion of horizons in pastoral practice, *see* my *Widening the Horizons*, chap. 3.

4. Normative Metaphors: Presence

1. For a social psychological analysis of narcissistic themes in contemporary American culture, *see* Christopher Lasch, *The Culture of Narcissism: American Life in an Age of Diminishing Expectations* (New York: W. W. Norton, 1978). For a more philosophical/historical perspective on the background of narcissism and the age of the self in Western thought, *see* David Pacini, *The Cunning of Modern Religious Thought* (Philadelphia: Fortress Press, 1987).
2. Max Weber, *The Protestant Ethic and the Spirit of Capitalism* (New York: Seabury Press, 1958).
3. For a cogent theological interpretation of the diversity of biblical understandings of faithful human response to the call of God, *see* Paul D. Hanson, *The Diversity of Scripture: A Theological Interpretation* (Philadelphia: Fortress Press, 1982).
4. For a useful development of a hermeneutics of pastoral actions, *see* Donald Capps, *Pastoral Care and Hermeneutics* (Philadelphia: Fortress Press, 1984).
5. For a thorough and provocative discussion of the tendency of twentieth-century pastoral practice to "bracket" moral/ethical concerns in favor of therapeutic expression of acceptance and forgiveness, *see* Don S. Browning, *The Moral Context of Pastoral Care* (Philadelphia: Westminster Press, 1976).
6. Samuel Terrien, *The Elusive Presence: Toward a New Biblical Theology* (San Francisco: Harper & Row, 1978).
7. Ibid., pp. 4-6.
8. Ibid., pp. 27, 28.
9. Ibid., p. 65.
10. Ibid., p. 66.
11. Ibid., p. 83.
12. Paul D. Hanson, *The People Called: The Growth of Community in the Bible* (San Francisco: Harper & Row, 1986), p. 102.
13. Terrien, *The Elusive Presence*, pp. 74, 75.
14. Hanson, *The People Called*, p. 404.
15. Jürgen Moltmann, *The Crucified God* (New York: Harper & Row, 1974), pp. 276-77.
16. John B. Cobb, Jr., *Theology and Pastoral Care* (Philadelphia: Fortress Press, 1977), p. 58.
17. Ibid., p. 59.
18. For further elaboration of the dialogical process involved in bringing about a "fusion of horizons" between contemporary life situations and biblical language and origins, *see* my *Widening the Horizons: Pastoral Responses to a Fragmented Society* (Philadelphia: Westminster Press, 1986).
19. E. Brooks Holifield, *A History of Pastoral Care in America* (Nashville: Abingdon Press, 1983).

5. Normative Metaphors: Community

1. Paul D. Hanson, *The People Called: The Growth of Community in the Bible* (San Francisco: Harper & Row, 1986), p. 33.

2. Ibid., p. 102.
3. For a clear and concise explication of the concept of an extended metaphor, *see* Sallie McFague, *Speaking in Parables* (Philadelphia: Fortress Press, 1975), p. 79. For further development of the use of extended metaphors in pastoral care and counseling, *see* my *Living Human Document* (Nashville: Abingdon Press, 1984), p. 170.
4. *Webster's New World Dictionary of the American Language*, Second College Edition (New York: World Publishing Co., 1974), p. 231.
5. Hanson, *The People Called*, pp. 43, 44.
6. Ibid., p. 243.

6. Normative Metaphors: Vocation

1. Karl Holl, "The History of the Word Vocation (Beruf)," Heber F. Peacock, trans., (unpub.), ET of Holl, "Die Geschichte des Worts Beruf," in *Gesammelte Aufsatze zur Kirchengeschichte*, vol. 3 (Tubingen: J. C. B. Mohr [Paul Siebeck], 1928), pp. 189-219, as referenced in James W. Fowler, *Faith Development and Pastoral Care* (Philadelphia: Fortress Press, 1987), p. 28.
2. Fowler, *Faith Development and Pastoral Care*, pp. 27-28.
3. Ibid., p. 28.
4. Ibid.
5. Ibid.
6. Gustaf Wingren, *The Christian's Calling: Luther on Vocation*, Carl C. Rasmussen, trans. (Edinburgh: Oliver and Boyd, 1958), pp. 4, 5.
7. Ibid., p. 46.
8. Ibid., p. 172. *See also* p. 182.
9. Ibid., p. 226.
10. David B. Guralnik, ed., *Webster's New World Dictionary of the American Language*, Second College Edition (Cleveland: World Publishing Co., 1972), p. 202.
11. Joseph L. Allen, *Love and Conflict: A Covenantal Model of Christian Ethics* (Nashville: Abingdon Press, 1984), p. 39.
12. William A. Beardslee, "Marriage as Covenant: Some Biblical and Theological Reflections" (Unpublished, privately distributed manuscript, 1980).
13. Cf., for example, such widely diverse sources as Walther Eichrodt, *Theology of the Old Testament*, vol. 1 (Philadelphia: Westminster Press, 1961); and Walter Brueggemann, "Covenanting as Human Vocation" in *Interpretation: A Journal of Bible and Theology*, vol. 33, no. 2, April 1979.
14. William A. Beardslee, "Marriage as Covenant," p. 6.
15. For a cogent and comprehensive discussion of marriage as vocation, *see* Joseph L. Allen, *Love and Conflict*, chap. 8.
16. Walter Brueggemann, "Covenanting as Human Vocation," pp. 110, 111.

BIBLIOGRAPHY

Allen, Joseph L. *Love and Conflict: A Covenantal Model of Christian Ethics*. Nashville: Abingdon Press, 1984.

Bellah, Robert, Richard Madsen, William M. Sullivan, Ann Swidler, and Steven M. Tipton. *Habits of the Heart: Individualism and Commitment in American Life*. Berkeley: University of California Press, 1985.

Browning, Don S. *The Moral Context of Pastoral Care*. Philadelphia: Westminster Press, 1976.

_____. *Religious Ethics and Pastoral Care*. Philadelphia: Fortress Press, 1983.

_____. *Religious Thought and the Modern Psychologies*. Philadelphia: Fortress Press, 1987.

Browning, Don S., ed., *Practical Theology: The Emerging Field in Theology, Church, and World*. San Francisco: Harper & Row, 1983.

Brueggemann, Walter. *The Prophetic Imagination*. Philadelphia: Fortress Press, 1978.

Capps, Donald. *Pastoral Care and Hermeneutics*. Philadelphia: Fortress Press, 1984.

Cobb, John B., Jr. *Theology and Pastoral Care*. Philadelphia: Fortress Press, 1977.

Eichrodt, Walther. *Theology of the Old Testament*, vol. 1. Philadelphia: Westminster Press, 1961.

Fowler, James W. *Faith Development and Pastoral Care*. Philadelphia: Fortress Press, 1987.

Gadamer, Hans-Georg. *Philosophical Hermeneutics*. Berkeley: University of California Press, 1976.

_____. *Reason in the Age of Science*. Cambridge: MIT Press, 1981.

_____. *Truth and Method*. New York: Crossroad, 1982.

Gerhart, Mary, and Allan M. Russell. *Metaphoric Process: The Creation of Scientific and Religious Understanding*. Fort Worth: Texas Christian University Press, 1984.

Gerkin, Charles V. *The Living Human Document: Re-Visioning Pastoral Counseling in a Hermeneutical Mode*. Nashville: Abingdon Press, 1984.

_____. *Widening the Horizons: Pastoral Responses to a Fragmented Society*. Philadelphia: Westminster Press, 1986.

Gilligan, Carol. *In a Different Voice*. Cambridge: Harvard University Press, 1982.

Hanson, Paul D. *The Diversity of Scripture: A Theological Interpretation*. Philadelphia: Fortress Press, 1982.

_____. *The People Called: The Growth of Community in the Bible*. San Francisco: Harper & Row, 1986.

Heschel, Abraham. *The Prophets*. New York: Harper & Row, 1962.

Holifield, E. Brooks. *A History of Pastoral Care in America: From Salvation to Self-Realization*. Nashville: Abingdon Press, 1983.

Holmes, Urban T., III. *Ministry and Imagination*. New York: Seabury Press, 1976.

Holton, Gerald. *Thematic Origins of Scientific Thought*. Cambridge: Harvard University Press, 1973.

Jacoby, Russell. *Social Amnesia*. Boston: Beacon Press, 1975.

Keller, Catherine. *From a Broken Web: Separation, Sexism, and Self*. Boston: Beacon Press, 1986.

Maslow, Abraham. *The Farther Reaches of Human Nature*. New York: Viking Press, 1971.

McConnell, Frank, ed. *The Bible and the Narrative Tradition*. New York: Oxford University Press, 1986.

McFague, Sallie. *Speaking in Parables*. Philadelphia: Fortress Press, 1975.

_____. *Metaphorical Theology: Models of God in Religious Language*. Philadelphia: Fortress Press, 1982.

_____. *Models of God: Theology for an Ecological, Nuclear Age*. Philadelphia: Fortress Press, 1987.

Metz, Johann Baptist. *Faith in History and Society: Toward a Practical Fundamental Theology*. New York: Seabury Press, 1980.

Moltmann, Jürgen. *The Crucified God*. New York: Harper & Row, 1974.

_____. *God in Creation: A New Theology of Creation and the Spirit of God*. London: SCM Press, 1985.

Niebuhr, H. Richard. *Radical Monotheism and Western Culture*. New York: Harper & Row, 1943.

_____. *Christ and Culture*. New York: Harper & Row, 1951.

_____. *The Responsible Self*. New York: Harper & Row, 1963.

Oates, Wayne E. *Pastoral Counseling in Social Problems: Extremism, Race, Sex, Divorce*. Philadelphia: Westminster Press, 1966.

_____. *Pastoral Counseling*. Philadelphia: Westminster Press, 1974.

Palmer, Parker. *The Company of Strangers: Christians and the Renewal of America's Public Life*. New York: Crossroad, 1985.

Reagan, Charles E., and David Stewart, eds. *The Philosophy of Paul Ricoeur*. Boston: Beacon Press, 1978.

Ricoeur, Paul. *The Rule of Metaphor: Multi-disciplinary Studies of the Creation of Meaning in Language*. Toronto: University of Toronto Press, 1975.

_____. *Essays in Biblical Interpretation*. Philadelphia: Fortress Press, 1980.

171

_____. *Interpretation Theory: Discourse and the Surplus of Meaning*. Fort Worth: Texas Christian University Press, 1976.

_____. *Time and Narrative*, vol. 1. Chicago: University of Chicago Press, 1984.

_____. *Time and Narrative*, vol. 2. Chicago: University of Chicago Press, 1985.

_____. *Time and Narrative*, vol. 3. Chicago: University of Chicago Press, 1988.

Rieff, Philip. *The Triumph of the Therapeutic: Uses of Faith After Freud*. New York: Harper & Row, 1966.

Rogers, Carl R. *Client-Centered Therapy*. Boston: Houghton Mifflin Co., 1951.

Ruether, Rosemary Radford. *Sexism and God-Talk: Toward a Feminist Theology*. Boston: Beacon Press, 1984.

Schon, Donald A. *The Reflective Practitioner: How Professionals Think in Action*. New York: Basic Books, 1983.

Schüssler Fiorenza, Elisabeth. *Bread Not Stone: The Challenge of Feminist Biblical Interpretation*. Boston: Beacon Press, 1986.

Terrien, Samuel. *The Elusive Presence: The Heart of Biblical Theology*. San Francisco: Harper & Row, 1978.

Tracy, David. *The Blessed Rage for Order*. New York: Seabury Press, 1975.

_____. *The Analogical Imagination*. New York: Seabury Press, 1978.

_____. *Plurality and Ambiguity: Hermeneutics, Religion, Hope*. San Francisco: Harper & Row, 1987.

Trible, Phyllis. *God and the Rhetoric of Sexuality*. Philadelphia: Fortress Press, 1978.

_____. *Texts of Terror: Literary-Feminist Readings of Biblical Narratives*. Philadelphia: Fortress Press, 1984.

Washington, James Melvin, ed. *A Testament of Hope: The Essential Writings of Martin Luther King, Jr.* San Francisco: Harper & Row, 1986.

Weber, Max. *The Protestant Ethic and the Spirit of Capitalism*. New York: Seabury Press, 1958.

Wingren, Gustaf. *The Christian's Calling: Luther on Vocation*. Edinburgh: Oliver and Boyd, 1958.

Aesthetic hermeneutics, 54, 63-64, 68-69
Aesthetic vision, 104
AIDS, 27-28, 127-28, 132
American individualism, 32
  psychological turn of, 33

Beardslee, William A., 151
Bellah, Robert, 14, 32
Black civil rights movement, 34, 37, 95
Boundary decision, 50
Browning, Don S., 19
Brueggemann, Walter, 70-71, 163

Calling, biblical meaning of, 144
Christian community
  centrifugal model of, 119-20,
      132-37
    location of pastor in, 137-42
  centripetal model of, 119-20, 135
    unintended consequences of,
        121-25
  leaven of, 137
    in family life, 139
    in neighborhood, 139-40
    in workplace, 140-42
Christian presence, 93
Christian narrative tradition, 16-17, 19, 158
Clinical pastoral education, 126, 132
Cobb, John B., Jr., 111-12
Common sense, 53-54, 65, 67, 80, 83, 92,
      118, 124-25, 150, 163
  power of, 63
  transformation of, 75
Community
  as normative metaphor, 117
  biblical tradition of, 123
  pastor's responsibility for, 118

safety of, 132
search for, 127-29
Contemporary religious language, poverty
    of, 111-12
Contract, historical image of, 149
Covenant
  biblical image of, 152-54
  contemporary complications of, 154-59
  making and breaking of, 159-61
Cult of personality, 119

Discernment, 71, 146
Dislocation, 126, 132, 135

Ecclesia, 144-45
Elusive presence, 106-8, 161-62
Exodus, 60

Feminist consciousness, 35, 37, 95
Feminist critique, 38
Finitude, 61
Fitting, 56, 59
Fowler, James W., 144
Fragmentation, 12, 29, 46, 94, 162
Fundamentalism, 40, 95, 125
Fusion of horizons, 19-20, 57

Gadamer, Hans-Georg, 19-21, 43-44, 47,
    54-57, 59, 62-64, 68-70, 76
Gerhart, Mary, 85
Gilligan, Carol, 39
God
  presence of, 106-10
  purpose of, 29
  wisdom of, 71

Hall, Karl, 144

Hanson, Paul, 134
Hebrew Bible, 60
Hermeneutics of suspicion, 19
Humanistic psychology, 34
Humanistic tradition
  See Tradition, humanistic

Imagistic wisdom
  See Wisdom, imagistic
Institutional loyalties, open marketplace of,
  122
Interpretive guidance, 68
Intuition in decision making, 51
Iran-Contra Affair, 27
Isaiah, 134-35

Jacoby, Russell, 31
James, William, 33
Judgment, wise, 59, 70, 78-79

Kant, Immanuel, 54, 69
Keller, Catherine, 38
King, Martin Luther, Jr., 35

Liberationist consciousness, 30
Living Human Document, 20, 46, 58
Luther, Martin, 145-46, 150

McFague, Sallie, 38
Mainline Protestantism, 33, 94, 125
Marital conflict, 36
Marketplace of values, 14
Marriage as covenant, 151-52
Metaphor, 16, 18, 83-84
  and pastoral care, 114
  biblical, 16, 18, 107, 111-12
  extended, 133
Metaphorical themata, 85-86, 92
Metaphorical theology, 22
Metaphorical wisdom, 111
Moltmann, Jürgen, 109
Moralism, 92, 100
Moral majority, 40

Narcissism, 92
Narrative hermeneutical practical theology,
  16
Narrative hermeneutics, 59
Native Americans, 35
Neighbor, meaning of, 52
Niebuhr, H. Richard, 56-57, 61-62, 69-70,
  72, 76, 125
Normative boundaries, questions about, 11
North American culture, 17

Oates, Wayne E., 81

Parish, meaning of, 124
Pastoral care and counseling, 21, 30, 46, 81
  psychologizing of, 114
Pastoral practice, context of, 48-49
Pastoral theological perspective, 46
Pastoral theology, 102
Paternalism, 29
Pluralism, 41
  among Christians, 94, 96
  of commitments, 155
  of cultures, 40
  of narratives, 158-59
Practical moral reasoning, 49
Practical theology, 13, 64-65
Prejudice, 20
Presence, normative vision of, 105-6
Priesthood of all believers, 118
Privatism, 100, 113
Prophetic imagination, 70
Prophetic ministry, 71, 74-76, 78, 80, 83,
  163
Prophets, 58, 70, 77, 80
Proverbs, 157
Psychoanalysis, 33

Quid pro quo, principle of, 149

Redemptive possibility, 105
Reflective practitioner, 55
Reframing, 12
Return to old-time values, 15
Ricoeur, Paul, 18, 21, 60-62
Rieff, Philip, 34
Rule of reason, 21
Russell, Allen M., 85

Salvific self-preoccupation, 151
Schon, Donald A., 55
Search for norms, 42
Secularization, 140
Self-interest, 149-50
Sexuality, 27-28
Sin, contemporization of meaning of, 112
Social contract theory, 149

Taste, 55-56, 64
Terrien, Samuel, 106-7
Theological education, 30
Tracy, David, 31
Tradition, 60, 93
  as historical process, 45
  as taken-for-granted way of life, 34
  biblical, 44-45, 106
  humanistic, 69
  Judeo-Christian, 43
  life in, 43-44

Roman Catholic, 118
Trible, Phyllis, 44-45

Vocation
as normative metaphor, 144
changes in meaning of, 145-47
Luther's definition of, 146
of Christian community, 154
of God, 147
of pastor, 163-64
secularization of meaning of, 147-49

Wall, Howard, 72
Weber, Max, 95
Widening the Horizons, 13-14, 20-21, 42, 46-47, 58-59, 68
Wilson, August, 116
Wisdom
biblical, 133-34
conflicts of, 157
imagistic, 111
traditional, 113